HIDDEN WAR

HOW SPECIAL OPERATIONS GAME WARDENS ARE RECLAIMING AMERICA'S WILDLANDS FROM THE DRUG CARTELS

BY LT. JOHN NORES, JR. [RET.]

FOREWORD BY CONGRESSMAN JARED HUFFMAN

Published by

Caribou Media Group, LLC
5600 W. Grande Market Drive, Suite 100
Appleton, WI 54913
Telephone: 920.471.4522

ISBN-13: 978-1-946267-61-0

Cover & Design by Jeromy Boutwell
Edited by Joe Shead

Printed in the United States of America

10 9 8 7 6 5 4 3 2 1

DEDICATION

For my brothers on the California Department of Fish and Wildlife's Marijuana Enforcement Team (MET). It is an honor to work with the most selfless, relentless, loyal, humble and dedicated team of special operators a man could ask for. Thanks for your constant fill-and-flow attitude and commitment to strengthening our thin green line.

PRAISE FOR HIDDEN WAR ...

"*Hidden War* is a riveting expose' of the egregious environmental catastrophe caused by drug cartels producing black-market marijuana. John Nores documents the unsung heroes who risk their lives to take on these well-armed, vicious groups."

LT.-COL. OLIVER NORTH
USMC (Ret.)
Host of American Heroes *on NRATV.Org*

Hidden War chronicles the development of the California Department of Fish and Wildlife's Marijuana Enforcement Team (MET). Most people have no idea why game wardens are involved in this battle to save the environment, but once you read about these encounters you will realize the total devastation to habitat and wildlife associated with illegal marijuana grows. Wildlife officers are uniquely qualified to work in this remote environment, and Lt. Nores details the dangers, excitement and rewards that go with the job.

MICHAEL P. CARION
Retired Chief, California Dept. of Fish and Wildlife — Law Enforcement Division

Gripping and gritty, *Hidden War* is a real-life thrill ride. Nores captures the dangers our wildlife law enforcement officials face every day. A compelling must-read on a persistent headline topic."

BRIG.-GEN. ANTHONY J. TATA
U.S. Army (Ret.)
National bestselling author of Dark Winter

"I had the pleasure of meeting Lt. Nores and his team during the filming of our documentaries; *Reclamation: The Battle for Terra Firma* and *War in the Woods.* Our team followed these professionals into America's backcountry and saw firsthand the carnage and devastation inflicted upon nature, wildlife and waterways by those involved in the illegal drug trade. Nores and his team of elite tactical operators dedicate their lives to public safety and the preservation of our most precious resources on a daily basis. *Hidden War* is masterfully written by a decorated thin green line warrior who has risked much to lead others under the most difficult circumstances and austere environments."

RICK STEWART
Host and Executive Producer
Patriot Profiles: Life of Duty *and* American Patriots: Unsung Heroes Magazine

"In the tradition of such courageous and legendary muckrakers as Upton Sinclair and Rachel Carson, Lt. John Nores exposes the story of illegal marijuana cultivation by the powerful drug cartels and the catastrophic effects they have on the environment. This gripping and incredibly researched page-turner is a must read for anyone concerned about the survival of our planet."

TOM GREENE
Writer, Producer, Director and Sportsman
Thunder in Paradise, Swamp Thing, *and* Magnum PI

"From the mist-laden haze of the Great Smokies to the Ozarks of the heartland, from remote reaches of New England to California, illegal cannabis cultivation has reached epidemic proportions. That's a travesty, a threat to the natural world we hold sacred and a mind-boggling intrusion into our country by drug cartels. In this carefully documented and well-written book, we get a microcosmic view of this appalling situation as it exists in California and what the 'thin green line' of wildlands law enforcement is doing to combat it. For those who care about the good Earth and harbor deep respect for the legacy of icons such as Theodore Roosevelt and John Muir, this book is at once a clarion call for continued action and an eye-opening must-read."

JIM CASADA, Ph.D.
Editor at Large
Sporting Classics Magazine

"If you think we aren't facing real, serious, threats to our natural resources from illicit drugs and human trafficking, you need to read *Hidden War*. It reads like the mission debrief from an action adventure novel, but it's not. *Hidden War* is the real, first-person story of battles being fought every day to save our wildlands from the ravages of criminals who don't give a damn about the land, the animals … or us."

JIM SHEPHERD
Publisher/Founder
The Outdoor Wire

"This is a fascinating look at a world the vast majority of people don't even know exists. For most who fish, hunt or recreate in the outdoors, game wardens are the ones who check licenses or issue a tag to someone who keeps a fish or two over the limit. But when vicious criminals steal and destroy public land and outdoor resources, game wardens are on the front lines, putting themselves in danger to protect the public. *Hidden War* is a compelling, exciting, and interesting look at the great people who do a very difficult job."

JEFF DAVIS
Editor
Whitetails Unlimited Magazine

I read books and scripts for a living and *Hidden War* is a must read. *Hidden War* tells the amazing and unknown story of a group of special operation game wardens and their never-ending war with the international drug cartels in California. This small elite team of earth warriors is up against an estimated eight to ten thousand cartel members, traffickers, and criminals. Not only do they take the fight to these bad guys, they protect California's wildlands and wildlife assets and prevent poisoned cannabis from hitting the national black market. Besides protecting the earth, water, and wildlife when taking down these violent criminals, they reclaim and restore the environmental damage done during these illegal activities. You'll find yourself unable to put the book down as you root for the good guys protecting what America holds dear."

DAVID SALZBERG
CEO and award-winning director and producer
Strong Eagle Media

TABLE OF CONTENTS

FOREWORD
BY CONGRESSMAN JARED HUFFMAN

California's North Coast is one of the most beautiful landscapes in the United States. Starting from the hidden beaches and rugged Pacific cliffs, you can follow its wild and scenic rivers up through coastal mountains, thickly forested with ancient redwoods. I am fortunate enough to represent California's 2nd Congressional District, which includes the entire length of the state's beautiful northern coastline, from Oregon down to the Golden Gate Bridge just north of San Francisco. Like so many of my constituents and visitors to our area, I look for any chance I can get to hike beneath the cool forest canopy or to fish for steelhead in icy, fast-moving waters. Congress is never so peaceful or quiet.

Yet the region's remoteness conceals some of its most disturbing environmental and public safety challenges: dewatered streams, polluted watersheds, illegally removed timber and safety hazards to wildlife, human visitors and downstream communities. This disturbing set of problems stems from a single cause: illegal marijuana-cultivation sites that have been established on remote private, tribal and state and federal public lands. Our region is home to California's so-called "Emerald Triangle" of Mendocino, Humboldt and Trinity counties — a rural, mountainous, heavily forested region covering approximately 10,000 square miles in northwestern California. Since the 1960s, this region has been at the core of our nation's cannabis trade — famous worldwide for its role in marijuana culture. This book is not about the historic "mom and pop" roots of the cannabis industry, however, but about our region's hidden secret as the national epicenter of illegal trespass marijuana grows.

I have long advocated for a more coherent federal and state policy on cannabis, in large part because the current grey market status is leading to acute environmental impacts on our forests. Decriminalization at a national level would mean bringing the industry out of the shadows, and out of the forests, so that those who want to grow and sell cannabis can do so in a transparent, lawful, environmentally conscious and seriously regulated way — just like any other crop or commodity.

In the meantime, as I work in Congress to convince my colleagues that our prohibition policy has been a failure and that we need to find better ways to manage this substance, I know that we need to do more to respond to the ongoing damage.

I gained a firsthand look at some of this devastation in August 2014 when I joined a law enforcement team and hiked into an illegal grow site in the Shasta-Trinity National Forest shortly after it was raided. I didn't need a formal assessment of the site to know the environmental damage was egregious and would be long-lasting. Besides all of the camp trash, propane bottles, human waste, fertilizers and a wide array of water-poisoning chemicals spread throughout the site, the growers had set up an irrigation system that completely diverted two tributaries of French Creek — a sensitive steelhead spawning area. This was during the height of the state's historic drought — the driest period in California's recorded history — meaning impacts downstream from the grow site would be even more pronounced. The damage was visible everywhere I looked: trees had been cut to open the canopy, and unregulated fertilizers, rodenticides and pesticides like the highly toxic Carbofuran were spread throughout the area.

In addition to the tons of fertilizer and poisons left at these sites, trespassers also leave behind miles of sophisticated irrigation works that can deplete seasonal streams and important tributaries, killing fish and wildlife and robbing downstream users of clean water. It is conservatively estimated that during that record drought, illegal trespass growers stole 1.3 billion gallons of water over just a single year (2013–2014). However, it is likely that there were far more water diversions, stream-flow reductions and watershed impacts from these clandestine grow sites than were ever found and remediated.

That operation to eradicate and reclaim a trespass grow site was one of many such missions conducted that summer by an inter-agency team that included staff from the California Department of Fish and Wildlife, the California Air National Guard's Counter Drug Task Force, environmental scientists from UC Davis, tribal officials and other allied law enforcement agencies. These varied entities came together under the threat posed by cartel growers to the land, endangered wildlife and waterways of the Emerald Triangle and North Coast region.

Shortly after that unforgettable trespass grow tour, I was pleased to learn of the California Department of Fish and Wildlife's (CDFW) proactive response to the trespass grow problem. In 2013, realizing that these operations threaten public safety while being responsible for some of the most devastating environmental crimes throughout the Golden State, the CDFW's Law Enforcement Division developed its first special operations tactical unit, the Marijuana Enforcement Team (MET), to target this problem.

The MET is the first dedicated team of this type in the agency's history, and it has paved the way for several additional cannabis-related enforcement groups to tackle the unique environmental compliance challenges of legal and illegal marijuana cultivation. CDFW MET officers focus on nothing else and run arrest, eradication and environmental-reclamation missions to protect wildlife and restore watersheds at as many grow sites as possible.

Congressman Huffman in a northern California DTO trespass marijuana cultivation complex in July 2014. Pictured left to right: Mark Higley of the Hoopa Tribe, two MET operators, Congressman Huffman, Dr. Mourad Gabriel and Dr. Gretta Wengert.

In this book, John Nores outlines the MET's development from its inception and details its work through a series of accounts of selected operations against the drug-trafficking organizations responsible for most trespass grows in California. CDFW MET officers, along with all the other law enforcement agents who help find and clean up these sites, take significant safety risks on the job, yet once the cases enter the courtroom, they can be difficult to prosecute and often result in minimal criminal penalties. That's why I authored a bipartisan bill in early 2014 that directed the U.S. Sentencing Commission to impose stiff penalties for individuals who cause environmental damage, such as clear-cutting trees, poisoning wildlife or damaging and diverting watersheds, while cultivating marijuana on trespass grows on private forest lands and federal public lands.

Despite bipartisan support in the House and Senate, the leadership of the House of Representatives did not take up the bill for consideration, so we worked directly with the U.S. Sentencing Commission, which has implemented new guidelines to increase criminal penalties for trespass marijuana grow operations. The Sentencing Commission correctly concluded that trespass grow operations deserve special attention because they "interfere with the ability of others to safely access and use the area and pose or risk a range of other harms, such as harms to the environment."

Because these trespass damages are now counted as separate or aggravating offenses, the criminal justice system has a new tool to respond to the environmentally harmful activities and to send a message that there are consequences not just for trespassing, but for the lasting downstream environmental harm caused by these grow sites. This change also means that the work of law enforcement teams like the MET can yield a legal outcome proportional to the risks they take when conducting their potentially dangerous operations.

As you read on, you will understand the extent of my concern, and hopefully share it with me. Law enforcement teams like the MET combat severe environmental crimes that take place far from the public eye. They are doing important and unheralded work, but they cannot solve this problem alone. Because of the pervasiveness of trespass grows throughout California and other parts of the nation, the heroic efforts described in this important new book deserve a robust and dedicated public policy response. ✼

INTRODUCTION

THE THIN GREEN LINE BECOMES SPECIAL OPS

BY LT. JOHN NORES, JR. [RET.]

> *"A spirit with a vision is a dream...*
> *with a mission."*
>
> — "Mission" by RUSH

My father, John Nores, Sr., was my hero. Because of his military service, passion for the shooting and conservation sports, and his incredible marksmanship skills, I wanted to be like him. My mother, an excellent shot and an equestrian, shared my father's affinity for the outdoors. Mom and Dad loved country, wildlife and wildland resources. They possessed a deep and abiding respect for "lives of service." They instilled that ethos in my three siblings and me from an early age. We were taught that anything worth doing is worth doing well, and to always protect and support those less fortunate.

Although Dad was a successful competitor in many shooting sports, his true passion was hunting and fishing. He hunted waterfowl and deer to feed our family, and he loved being in the outdoors at all hours. With his help, I passed my hunter safety class at age 9, and was target shooting and hunting small game and waterfowl before I was a pre-teen. Watching sunrises and sunsets while hunting the West Coast's beautiful backcountry was one of my favorite activities to share with my dad and uncle while growing up. During those magical outdoor moments, Dad would always tell me, "The woods are my church." Never before or since have so few words meant so much. What I didn't realize at the time was that these first hunting experiences with my father were a catalyst for my lifelong love of the outdoors and the desire to explore, enjoy and protect it.

When my parents were away, I was responsible for — as they called it — their "Wolf Pack." As the oldest, I was the designated alpha, making sacrifices to ensure my siblings were safe and had what they needed (a mindset that has served me well into adulthood and a life of public service).

When I was a teenager, Dad introduced me to handloading rifle and handgun cartridges. I was hooked. He taught me the intricacies of handloading methods, driving home the creed of safety, patience and perfection when crafting precision hunting and target loads. I created loads for my first deer rifle (a used Remington Model 600 chambered in .243 Win.) when I was 16. That rifle, coupled with a precision handload, was the combination I used to harvest my first California black-tailed deer and my first Montana whitetail buck. The combination would serve me well for decades.

GOING PROFESSIONAL

In 1987, I completed freshman classes in Criminal Justice Administration at San Jose State University. After meeting a California game warden six months prior on a remote backcountry trip, I felt compelled to take up that profession. Given my love for the outdoors and our country's wildlife resources, I chose to protect wildlife and public safety. That random encounter with a game warden, coupled with Dad's influence, contributed heavily to my decision, and I knew that it was God's plan for me.

After completing my Bachelor of Science at San Jose State University, the California Department of Fish and Wildlife placed me on a waiting list. I entered the master's program, once again focusing on Criminal Justice Administration to aid my dream career. In January 1992, I received a call from the CDFW. I was elated. I was hired as a probationary game warden cadet and would start the seven-month law enforcement academy the following month. That was 28 years ago, and my career path has been a blessed, exciting and challenging blur ever since.

Over those 28 years, I've been fortunate to work in every area of wildlife law enforcement throughout California. My career was incredibly diverse. I've served as a patrol warden, enforcing hunting and fishing regulations and ensuring public safety in inland districts throughout southern California and around my hometown in Silicon Valley. I also worked marine patrol off the California coast, as well as statewide undercover commercial wildlife and anti-poaching operations.

However, the most dangerous, environmentally relevant work I've done took place during the final 14 years of my career.

LAYING THE FOUNDATION

In my cadet academy, I was selected as one of four squad leaders, responsible for making sure my squad mates were in tip-top shape for the academic, physical and tactical challenges we faced daily during the curriculum. I gave it my all. Flashbacks of looking after my siblings during our childhood Wolf Pack days resonated with me throughout the academy, and I realized my parents groomed me for this role from the start.

Within a few years of graduating the academy and becoming a solo warden working my assigned district, I became a firearms instructor, defensive tactics instructor and Field Training Officer (FTO). I was selected as my region's Firearms and Defensive Tactics Committee member, evaluating and developing firearms, tactical-training and arrest-and-control tactics for the entire Law Enforcement Division (LED). My background in firearms, ballistics, arrest-and-control techniques, high-risk indoor entry and hunting and stalking tactics proved helpful to my tasks.

While developing as a leader and trainer within my agency, I networked all over the Bay Area with skilled tactical teams and SWAT units. Along with my game warden squad mate, Markos, we attended SWAT, sniper, carbine, submachine gun, handgun and tactical-tracking classes to gain the skills and knowledge needed to bring these advanced tactics to the California Department of Fish and Wildlife's (CDFW) Law Enforcement Division (LED).

Prior to working with us, our allied law enforcement agency brothers and sisters had never worked with game wardens on a tactical level, and they began taking us seriously as professional, tactically savvy operators. Our game wardens ran into more violent encounters with armed and dangerous felons than ever before. The incidents often took place in remote areas, hours away from backup. The timing couldn't have been better.

In 2003 and 2005, I was selected to be the Recruit Training Officer (RTO) for two of our cadet-training academies in Napa and Asilomar. During those assignments, I was the first-line supervisor and go-to guy for approximately 30 cadets going through the same stressful curriculum I completed more than a decade prior. These were great assignments that prepared me well for my promotion to patrol lieutenant in June 2005.

Shortly after my promotion, I traveled to Cambodia with a fellow special operations lieutenant to teach wildlife officers in southeast Asia overt and covert commercial wildlife-investigation skills. The two-week class marked the first time our agency's game wardens had gone overseas to teach or operate.

THE DAY THAT CHANGED EVERYTHING

Within a month of becoming the squad supervisor for three counties around Silicon Valley, my career path changed forever. August 5, 2005, marked the longest, most challenging day of my career.

That morning, two other game wardens and I assisted the Santa Clara County Sheriff's Office Marijuana Eradication Team with an allied-agency arrest-and-eradication operation on a Mexican drug cartel's marijuana grow in the densely wooded mountains above Silicon Valley. While stalking into the grow complex, a heavily armed crew of cartel gunmen ambushed us. Although the gunmen only got one shot off before we neutralized them, that one shot hit my young partner through both legs, causing massive damage and blood loss. It was agonizing. I kept him alive and out of shock during the three-hour wait for an air rescue, and I was unsure if he would survive the gunfight. We were blessed that he survived and recovered to become one of the most distinguished game wardens in our force today.

That gunfight catalyzed the egregious environmental destruction drug cartels wreak throughout California and other parts of our great nation. They poison pristine waterways, kill wildlife and threaten outdoor enthusiasts. With game wardens on the jurisdictional forefront of protecting wildlife resources and public safety, especially in remote areas, it was time for us to make neutralizing this threat a priority.

FIGHTING BACK

During the eight years that would follow, all of the leadership, tactical training, operational experience and relationships I built with domestic law enforcement and military special operations units would pay off.

In 2013, I was privileged to co-found, develop and lead the nation's first, full-time, special operations marijuana-enforcement unit, the CDFW's Marijuana Enforcement Team (MET). The statewide team excels in hunting and apprehending DTO growers with the help of specialized, life-saving K9s. Without district boundaries and administrative red tape, we can respond anywhere and at any time.

Although focused on combating illegal trespass marijuana-cultivation operations, MET is our agency's go-to tactical unit for high-risk public safety missions anywhere in the state. Within MET, I developed our first sniper team — a key component to our agency's enhanced tactical capabilities. Known as Delta Team, it's trained to operate day or night and can sustain operations anywhere in the state without support or resupply for several days.

THE THIN GREEN LINE

The MET is up against a formidable threat. Mexican drug trafficking organizations (DTOs) embed throughout the country to run their criminal activities. Tens of thousands of cartel operatives smuggled across the U.S.-Mexico border don't only grow poisoned marijuana on our nation's wildlands. They also operate human trafficking, the manufacture and distribution of methamphetamine, gun running to fuel the cartel wars a plethora of other crimes.

The cartels recently added specialized, one-way Panga boats designed to navigate around the Gulf of Mexico and up the West Coast to deliver processed marijuana, methamphetamine and people. These camouflaged boats hide from aerial surveillance and can carry large loads. Additionally, they coordinate activities with overseas terrorist groups.

I have never seen a more environmentally destructive criminal element in 28 years of protecting our country's wildlife resources.

Given the threat, we advanced our tactics, training and operational protocols to combat the cartels effectively. Since that pivotal August day in 2005, our team members sustained four more officer-involved shootings with violent cartel growers. The encounters highlighted the need for a highly trained, well-equipped team.

LOOKING BACK

Now, following a diverse and rewarding career, I reflect on every opportunity and experience I've been blessed to have throughout this journey. I'm lucky to have a handful of growth-minded leaders over the last three decades who supported and mentored me.

I've had the most dedicated, selfless and supportive teammates a man can ask for; operators so team-oriented, humble, skilled and selfless that I'm proud to call them brothers. The bonds we've built together last a lifetime and we are truly a family. I have my father and mother's family heritage of service to community and country to thank for that.

My dad passed away in May 2013 after a long fight with cancer, just three months shy of his 70th birthday. We spent the last days of his life shedding tears of joy and sorrow as we reflected on many years of hunting and shooting together, along with my career highlights, of which he was immensely proud. Shortly after his passing, my sister, Laura, created a memorial for him and his legacy on our wilderness sanctuary that he loved so much. I visit it often throughout the year, missing him every day. And when walking in the high country, I feel his presence with every step. The woods are my church and I'm grateful for the love, guidance and support Dad and Mom gave us Wolf Packers to do what we do best: pay it forward and protect and serve. ✻

Laura Nores' hand-carved wilderness memorial for John Nores, Sr. — "The woods are my church."

N 37 05' 04"
W 121 14' 04"

CHAPTER 01

CARTEL KINGPIN IN SILICON VALLEY: 15 YEARS TO JUSTICE

"He will win who, prepared himself, waits to take the enemy unprepared."

— The Art of War, by Sun Tzu

NOVEMBER 1998 – MACHADO CREEK – SOUTH SILICON VALLEY FOOTHILLS

Debbie Gregg was the perfect, and unfortunate, example of what's at stake in this war. Debbie made her home in this part of California for the same reasons many people do. The natural beauty is unparalleled. With Uvas Reservoir not far over the ridge to the west, and the Machado Creek flowing through her parcel, Debbie enjoyed the migrating raptors and waterfowl that flew over her house during the fall months. Deer, wild pigs and turkeys fed routinely in her sanctuary. In the spring, threatened steelhead trout used the creek to spawn after their arduous journey from the Pacific Ocean.

It was paradise, except for one thing.

Since purchasing land nearby a year earlier, Debbie's neighbor, "J.R.," developed his property at the expense of the natural beauty. He destroyed wildlife habitat and bulldozed through the sensitive creek. Confronting him about the environmental destruction only exacerbated the situation. J.R. threatened that he could make Debbie disappear any time he wanted.

Regardless, it was clear the water and wildlife couldn't handle any more disturbances. So Debbie did what most people would do: she called the authorities.

A game warden from the California Department of Fish & Wildlife, Markos, soon paid her a visit. After hearing her account, Markos explained how unsanctioned streambed alterations can be both civil and criminal offenses. He told her he would investigate further. Help for the creek, it seemed, was finally on its way.

However, Debbie wouldn't get the chance to see her beloved wilderness revived. She'd crossed a dangerous line, and she paid for it with her life. Debbie was found dead of a gunshot wound near the creek on J.R.'s side of the fence.

The investigation that ensued resulted in first-degree murder charges for J.R. A "lying in wait" enhancement added to the charges, and the jury convicted him in September 2000. J.R. received a life sentence in prison. It wouldn't last. He would spend less than a decade behind bars.

J.R.'s first appeal was denied, but the California Supreme Court overturned the conviction in a bizarre twist of events in late 2009. The court concluded that the jury's visit to the murder scene was improper because it took place during the original trial's deliberation period.

J.R. returned to Silicon Valley as a free man, and things quickly deteriorated from there. In late summer 2010, sheriff's deputies responded to a shots-fired call near midnight on the ridge above J.R.'s property. Deputies found a dead man and several AK-47 shell casings. Although originally described as a "sheepherder," the dead man was anything but, with no sheep present in an area that was too steep, brushy and rocky for sheep to graze. Coincidentally, officials spotted numerous marijuana plants on the parcel.

The murder underscored the truth about J.R.'s property: he was running a clandestine marijuana-cultivation operation.

And that's where my story starts. The following season, we started a targeted, allied-agency investigation into J.R.'s property.

APRIL 2011 – SLEEPY VALLEY ROAD – SOUTH SILICON VALLEY FOOTHILLS

Concealed in several layers of bank vegetation and tree canopy above Machado Creek, Spag, Hunter and I sat silently in our listening post/observation post (LP/OP). As the dense fog lifted, we made out the shape of our surveillance target 100 yards away — a new gate. This marked the entrance

Undocumented cash seized during the follow-up to the Tohara Canyon and Sleepy Valley grow complex operation.

to J.R.'s multi-million-dollar black-market marijuana-cultivation complex. We knew it was a choke point for vehicles and an ideal spot to see the faces of the individuals responsible. Our observations were critical to success.

Our hide was ideal — the handiwork of three rural ops snipers. Cloaked in shade throughout the day, it offered multiple escape trails behind us. This afforded more than a tactical advantage. We needed an exit in case we were compromised, or worse, taking fire from J.R.'s minions.

I tapped Spag's boot with mine, signaling that I was going off optics and moving position. After being frozen in place for more than two hours, I needed to stretch. Spag acknowledged by nodding slowly, never taking his eyes off the target. With Spag and Hunter focused on the gate and the surrounding area below, I turned around and monitored our back trail. I shook off the morning chill and reflected on the day's operation, my allied-agency teammates just inches away and the whirlwind of changes we had all experienced over the last six years.

Significant change took place within our Santa Clara County allied-agency Marijuana Enforcement Team (MET) since 2010. Snake and Rails, my first two allied-agency partners from the sheriff's office MET, rotated off their assignments in late 2010 and were replaced by Spag and Hunter. A veteran sergeant within the sheriff's office, Spag had just transferred to team leader of his agency's MET in late 2010. During the transition, Spag stepped down from running his agency's sniper team, realizing that overseeing the MET required all his attention. This was exciting, as Spag and I had already been decades-long colleagues and friends.

I met Spag in my first sniper school, hosted by his agency in 2001. He was a young, motivated, disciplined, generous and highly organized (affectionately considered OCD by many fellow operators) deputy then. I shared the same characteristics as a young state game warden trying to make a difference at home in Santa Clara County. We hit it off instantly. Together with my young game warden partner and friend, Markos, Spag noticed the motivation and skill sets we showed during that precision shooting school. As we got to know each other, and other snipers from all over the state during class, Spag commented that we were the first game wardens he had seen in any tactical shooting school and was impressed that we had bought and built our own rifles on our own time and at our own expense.

While many of the federal, state, and local law enforcement officers and U.S. military special operations sniper team members in attendance seemed puzzled by our presence, Spag was just the opposite. He embraced us as equals.

Spag was one of the first allied-agency spec ops brothers to see the tactical progression and skill of California game wardens and was instrumental in promoting our first equal partnership and unified mission. Over the next decade, Spag and I worked many tactical operations together and reworked and improved our agency's basic sniper school. Following that, we developed the Silicon Valley's first advanced sniper school and began teaching courses to law enforcement and military snipers all over the West Coast.

However, Spag and I agree our best years together were 2011–2013, when we were immersed in working MET operations together. As two team leaders, we had honed one of the most effective and progressive allied-agency drug trafficking organization (DTO) fighting tactical teams in California. Those developments, coupled with numerous violent-suspect apprehensions on many dangerous missions together, solidified a lifelong bond and brotherhood.

A generation younger than Spag and me, Hunter was a motivated, quick-witted, direct, yet soft-spoken deputy with a love of hunting, fishing and all things outdoors. We all appreciated his dry sense of humor. I'd met Hunter many years earlier while on ATV patrol, when he and members of his family were hunting a mountainous area outside Silicon Valley. Hunter and those in his party were conservationists and all were friendly — a solo game warden's ideal field contacts.

Hunter and I stayed in touch after that random field contact and reconnected in the 1990s when he was in high school doing ride-alongs with local law enforcement agencies. Hunter was more of a partner than a ride-along that day, helping me with surveillance. I liked him immediately, and together we detected numerous angling and hunting violations. Knowing he would make a great game warden, I was disappointed a few years later to hear he had joined the sheriff's office. Our loss was their gain. I didn't expect to work with him directly much in the future.

When Spag and his command staff asked me to participate in the oral board-examination process for their agency's new MET position in early 2011, I jumped at the chance. Knowing that the deputy selected would work with Spag and our game wardens, this was a great opportunity. I was happy to see Hunter testing for the MET deputy position and was even more pleased to know we would be working together when he got the job.

Back at the hide, Hunter tapped my back and whispered, "Movement below. Black pickup truck with a water tank in the bed and … an animal cage?"

I turned slowly, raised my binoculars and scanned the gate. We could make out the faces of the two men, as well as the items in the truck's bed. Spag took down the license plate number as Hunter and I continued to scan for details.

The water tank was huge: a 10,000-gallon black-polymer tank commonly used on marijuana-cultivation sites. At the base of the tank, I spotted a gas-powered water pump and the animal cage Hunter had mentioned. I was shocked to see what was inside.

"That's a bobcat," Hunter whispered. "Who pens up and transports a wild bobcat? Who does that?"

I shook my head in disgust. We refocused when the truck stopped at the gate and both men exited to unlock the heavy chain and padlock. The Hispanic men in their late 20s or early 30s dressed in earth-tone clothing. The passenger carried a sheathed, fixed-blade knife on his belt. Both men carried holstered pistols on their right hips. This wasn't a typical ranch work crew.

After clearing the gate, the truck was up the road and out of view in seconds. We waited another two hours before the truck returned and exited the property. Not surprisingly, the water tank, water pump and caged bobcat were all missing.

Over the next two months, we monitored and documented approximately 10 different men coming onto the property, with only a fraction of them coming out and leaving the ranch. Several more water tanks, water pumps and many miles of spooled black irrigation poly pipe were also delivered and left on the property. The activity illustrated the magnitude of J.R.'s operation. Although all these observations were critical to building the case, we had not yet identified J.R. — the plaza boss himself — on the property or associated him with the grow operation. Frustrated, we continued to grind out surveillance details, confident we'd get lucky and place the kingpin on the property.

Our luck changed the following week when we saw the same black truck approach the gate. This time, J.R. sat in the passenger seat. He got out to look around as his driver opened the gate. Another big black water tank was in back, along with a large stack of 50-pound fertilizer bags, some new backpack irrigation sprayers and more black poly pipe. We watched as J.R. directed his driver where to go and what to do once they cleared the gate, making it obvious who was in charge. With the gate closed and the truck now up the canyon and out of view, we all looked at each other and smiled, silently celebrating the day's turning point in the case. J.R. exposed himself as not only having knowledge of the grow operation on his property, but he also showed us he was calling the shots. A 60-second window of magnified surveillance after several days and hundreds of hours had paid off, and now he was ours.

Over the next few months, we gained more intel on J.R.'s grow operation, assessing what we were up against and what we needed for the takedown. We also discovered he ran multiple overt and covert grow sites on his and a neighboring property.

Debbie wouldn't get the chance to see her beloved wilderness revived. She'd crossed a dangerous line, and she paid for it with her life. Debbie was found dead of a gunshot wound near the creek on J.R.'s side of the fence.

Additional ground and air surveillance revealed a fresh, heavily used foot trail going from J.R.'s northern property border into Tohara Canyon and onto his neighbor's large, heavily wooded hunting ranch. J.R. brought in additional DTO growers to expand his enterprise and develop two additional complexes on the neighboring ranch. The new site also bordered Uvas Reservoir — a drinking water reserve for Silicon Valley and a fishery for threatened steelhead, adding to the negative impacts of the additional grow site.

I had worked with this neighboring landowner over the previous 15 years, handling numerous poaching, trespassing and night-hunting/spotlighting cases. He became furious when we told him about the grows on his property. We agreed these sites needed to be raided as soon as possible.

After spotting this new trail, we conducted additional overflights of both properties to gather the final details needed for a takedown of the entire operation. During the overflight, Spag located the two grow complexes on J.R.'s ranch, both located deep in two separate canyons. These grows were cut out of very dense

It's not just the marijuana that chokes out pristine wilderness areas. The camps that support the grows are full of toxic garbage. This is the polluted camp and kitchen near the first Tohara Canyon DTO grow site.

vegetation on two steep hillsides. A red cross topped with white signs marked each, identifying them as legal medicinal grows to any aircraft. Regardless, we were certain these grows were being irrigated by illegally diverted water from the sensitive streams below. We also suspected the large black water tanks we'd seen were caches for stolen water from these creeks as well.

Following the overflight, we had everything we needed for the takedown. Since the operation involved at least four grow complexes spread out over large distances on two properties, we faced numerous challenges. We needed to hit all four sites as quickly as possible on raid day for officer safety, to prevent evidence destruction and to keep the suspects from escaping. Given the murders associated with this case and the violent nature of DTO cultivation groups in general, we weren't taking any chances. Having already been involved in three gunfights with DTO growers throughout Santa Clara County, we needed a solid plan with an abundance of skilled operators to pull it off safely.

So many moving parts raised concern. As any law enforcement or military special operations professional knows, the more complicated the mission, the more resources needed. And the more resources needed, the more likely it is that something will go sideways. Murphy's Law tends to derail the best plan, especially large-scale, multi-team operations like this one. Over the next few weeks, Spag, Hunter and I worked carefully to bring the team together, secure the air and ground assets needed, and develop the best contingency plan to keep Mr. Murphy out of the mission entirely.

JULY 2011 – MACHADO CREEK – SOUTH SILICON VALLEY FOOTHILLS

On raid day, a large mix of skilled operators stood ready to go. With four grow sites to hit, our plan involved breaking down into two apprehension and eradication teams to handle all four grow sites simultaneously. In a pre-dawn briefing, our group reviewed the operational timeline, team assignments, infiltration and exfiltration logistics, and contingency plans, should things go wrong.

I followed up by giving another presentation on grow site health and safety hazards, explaining the dangers of the operation beyond the potential of armed growers. Since our previous three officer-involved shootings in 2005, 2008, and 2010, officer safety and public health threats became more common throughout DTO trespass grow sites. Anti-personnel booby traps (Vietnam-era punji pits, snare wire traps, covered and hidden deep pit traps, etc.) also needed to be addressed, as did the potential of EPA-banned poisons and other toxic substances. With DTO growers smuggling highly poisonous, toxic and deadly nerve agent-based insecticides (Furadan, Carbofuran, Metafos and similar poisons under different trade names) into the United States from Mexico to use throughout their grow sites, our entry team members needed to be extremely careful.

Dispersed throughout the site's water source and sprayed directly onto the leaves and buds of the marijuana plants, these poisons instantly kill any animal that ingests them. Trespass growers often mix the pink liquid poison into open food cans to kill any wildlife entering the grow site. Large numbers of the western United States' most sensitive wildlife species (mountain lions, black bears, gray foxes, mule deer, golden eagles, steelhead, Pacific fishers, etc.) are poisoned in thousands of DTO grow sites each year, and if any of our MET operators ingested even a small quantity of these poisons, the results could be fatal. Even DTO growers themselves know the dangers of these poisons, calling them *"el Diablo"* (the Devil).

Our teams planned to hit all four grows (two in Sleepy Valley and two around Tohara Canyon on the hunting ranch) on foot at first light, allowing a stealthy approach for maximum apprehension success. Hunter headed up the largest team of operators — all deputies from the sheriff's office — to handle the Sleepy Valley grow sites on J.R.'s parcel. That site was confirmed to have several structures to clear, in addition to a large grow complex, and a big team was needed to handle it safely. Once that site was secured, Hunter would send some of his team to assist Spag and I on the trespass grow sites next door on the hunting ranch.

Our plans in place, we started the operation.

Spag and I headed up a smaller nine-operator team to raid the Tohara hunting ranch grow sites. Even with 18 operators involved in all four raids, we needed to be efficient, as all four grows were surely live-in sites, with suspects working and living 24/7 within the complex. And with all four sites spread out over several canyons of mountainous terrain, we needed to get lucky.

We gained access to the hunting ranch's northern grow site through a break-off path from the Tohara site trail. We split our team there. On point and moving our team slowly and silently, Spag stopped us at the trail junction as we all took a knee. With our team's visual presence minimized, we remained silent, moving only our camouflaged faces and shadowed eyes to scan the

The poisons used at illegal grow sites are, not surprisingly, also illegal. The banned chemicals in this backpack irrigation sprayer could kill wildlife, contaminate water supplies, devastate the local ecology and linger for years. The growers don't care. Protecting the environment is at the bottom of their list.

wooded terrain around the trail. Positioned right behind Spag with my M14 up at the high ready, I peered over my iron sights and scanned the right side of the trail. After a few minutes of silence, with no threats detected, and now confident we were alone on the trail, Spag signaled the northern grow site raid team to break off. That team required a longer hike to its target, so the three of us held in place to give the operators a head start.

Essentially a preliminary scout team of three, they would stalk above the grow site, and hold and monitor it from the ridge above. The scout team would move in when more support personnel arrived. The northern hunting ranch grow was located deep in a box canyon, and we banked on the grower not having cell phone coverage from within it. Realistically, both the Sleepy Valley and the southern hunting ranch grow sites would be secure before we commenced the final raid of the day in this remote area. If compromised before we cleared it, the growers could bail and hide before we arrived. Worse, they could be armed and waiting to ambush us.

Given his solid fieldcraft skills and extensive experience on MET ops, Rails, a sheriff's office sergeant we first worked with in 2004, headed up the three-man team. He gave me a thumbs-up and led his team down the trail.

Our team held in place for another 15 minutes, carefully watching the trail ahead. Once Rails' team was well on its way, and the pre-sunrise light around us shined bright enough to assess threats ahead clearly, we moved out. Spag kept our pace slow and our movement stealthy, always trying to maintain the element of surprise. The growers' camp area was farther down the trail, as aerial surveillance had revealed. With thick brush and a dense tree canopy throughout the canyon ahead making an ideal spot for a camp and kitchen area, we anticipated finding the growers' camp soon.

Five yards behind Spag, I looked back to check on our team. Behind me was Quinn, a young game warden and recent addition to my patrol squad. I could see the excitement and intensity in his eyes as he focused on his stalk. Quinn moved carefully and silently along the trail, rolling his feet heel to toe, carefully picking and placing his steps ahead. Behind Quinn was Miya, with R.D. at the tail gunner position covering our back trail.

We stalked up the trail into a large canyon, slowly gaining elevation. With our GPS units showing the grow less than 200 yards ahead, we scanned for signs of the camp. The surrounding terrain changed from a well-worn path through a grass-covered meadow paralleling the creek to a weaving route through dense tree cover and coyote brush. We registered the change and sensed we were close. Trespass growers routinely bury their camp and kitchen areas in dense terrain to hide them from ground and aerial surveillance. With visibility ahead limited to 15 yards in the pre-dawn light, our excitement peaked.

Spag stopped mid-step. His AR-15's barrel and eyes locked ahead. I slowly moved up to assess. Candy wrappers, cigarette butts and some black irrigation pipe hardware pieces lay scattered on the ground, a sign we were close to bumping into growers just waking up in camp. I squeezed Spag's shoulder with my support hand — the silent signal we were ready to move on.

Like drifting smoke, we moved farther down the trail, weaving through the brush. Pushing through a final vegetation line, Spag spotted our target: a camouflaged tent and a kitchen area set up in a tree-covered meadow just 25 yards ahead. Still early and a few minutes before sunrise, the camp remained still and silent.

We took a knee at the edge of the meadow and assessed the camp ahead. Clearing tents is dangerous and challenging. By contrast, clearing buildings on high-risk entry operations at least provides some level of cover with solid walls and construction framing. With tents, the tight spaces between operators and suspects, and the thin nylon walls, can make assaults deadly.

Breaking cover, Spag stalked to the left of the first tent, as Quinn and I worked to the right. Miya and R.D. fanned out wide on both sides of the tent to cover us and prevent a blue-on-blue crossfire disaster in the event we had to engage.

A second before we announced ourselves, Quinn and I spotted movement inside. Just waking up, and clueless to our presence just a few feet away, the groggy grower raised his head for an early morning stretch. Peering through the skylight screen and expecting to see an empty and silent camp, his eyes widened in shock as he focused on the muzzle brake of Quinn's M1A pointed at his head at point-blank range. Before the grower could even think about reaching for his gun, Quinn ordered him to put his hands up as Spag and I pounced into the tent to handcuff and secure him.

Spag radioed Hunter and informed him we were code 4 (safe and secure) with one man in custody. Hunter responded with his own good news: his team had two suspects in custody after hitting the Sleepy Valley complexes effectively at first light. Surprising both growers sleeping in their camper, Hunter's team breached the door and cleared the structure in seconds. Both growers were pulled from their beds and in handcuffs before they could grab three loaded guns on a nearby table. Behind the camper in a makeshift wire pen were the remains of the bobcat we observed several months earlier. Killed some time before raid day, the bobcat was skinned, stretched and displayed on the fence like some sick trophy. Disgusted, we'd later push to add illegal possession of a furbearer and animal cruelty charges to the stack of criminal charges these men would face.

With Hunter's sites secure and his team heavy on operators, we formed a quick plan to double-time some of his guys to our location and secure our

Diverting creeks is one method illegal growers use to irrigate their crops. Here, Quinn assesses the Tohara Canyon grow site's water diversion and impoundment.

suspect for transport to jail. Within 15 minutes, two deputies from Hunter's team reached our camp and began escorting our suspect out of the canyon.

Eager to proceed to the hunting ranch's southern grow complex, we were finally ready to move. Now back in our original stack, Spag led us past the camp and up the trail to locate and secure the grow site. Before stepping off, I looked around the camp's kitchen area and noticed two squirrel carcasses hanging in the kitchen area. Wildlife crimes incense game wardens, and these mammals were killed without a license and well outside of the legal hunting season.

That's to say nothing of the trash. Cooking waste, propane bottles, fertilizers and pesticide containers littered the camp. Two backpack sprayers in the kitchen area likely contained banned pink poisons common to DTO operations. We used extra caution to steer clear of these containers. Our disgust didn't end there. A few steps away, I found toilet paper and human excrement in the small creek behind the camp. Infuriating.

Less than a quarter-mile up the canyon, we found the first sign of the grow. What should have been a flowing creek along the trail was a bone-dry wash. The brushy trail opened onto a steep hillside covered in marijuana plants as far as the eye could see. Positioned on the south-facing slope, the grow angled to give J.R.'s sunlight-hungry cash crop maximum sun exposure. The grows contained at least 5,000 marijuana plants and were covered in a labyrinth of well-worn trails spider-webbing in all directions. The trail complex allowed growers easy access to each plant, as well as paths to the bottom of the mountain or the top of the ridge where the grow terminated. Numerous escape routes cut across the complex. Because we were at the bottom and would have to clear it uphill, the growers would have the tactical advantage if any waited in ambush.

We stalked and scanned uphill, clearing the grow site foot by foot. Quinn spotted the complex's water source. Behind a plywood and timber dam stood a black plastic-lined pool positioned in the middle of the drainage. A gasoline-powered water pump with a hose system attached to the edge of the dam. Now the dry creek and stripped-out bank vegetation along the trail below us made sense. This crew used the pump to impound the channel's water and cut off all creek flow. They used the makeshift pool to irrigate the surrounding plants.

For the next 30 minutes, we cleared the grow site, passing a mix of poisons, fertilizers, irrigation tools, a small kitchen and two marijuana-processing areas before reaching the end of the complex. At the top of the ridge, we did a position check and mapped our location. Concealed on top of the tree-covered ridge dividing the hunting ranch's north and south grow complexes was a well-worn trail going north and downhill just 20 yards ahead. Descending toward the northern grow site, this trail had to be an artery between the north and south grows. Realizing we had just found the mother lode, Spag and I looked at each other and nodded, agreeing we had a tactical advantage and an unplanned opportunity.

Spag radioed Rails and requested a SITREP (situational report). Rails informed us that support operators from Hunter's team had arrived and were now in position on the eastern ridgeline above the grow. With eyes on the edge of the complex below, his team heard muted, Spanish-speaking voices in the canyon just after first light. Rails stressed that it sounded like several growers starting their day.

Now an hour after sunrise, everything woke up. Raptors flew overhead and sounded off, while smaller birds buzzed by on the ground. Jet traffic from San Jose International Airport disrupted the morning peace.

Before Spag gave the green light to converge on the grow complex, we discussed our next steps. With the only suspect in the Tohara south site now in custody, and all the growers in both Sleepy Valley sites also captured without injuries, we were ahead of the game. Now we needed to complete the final and most challenging part of the operation.

Murphy's Law hadn't compromised any phase of the day's mission, and we needed to keep it that way. During mission planning, we stressed the need to catch every grower on the grounds. Besides team morale and pride, the deterrence effect of complete success against J.R.'s crew to other DTO groups when this story spread was critical. And given the sinister background of this case, Debbie's murder demanded it.

Spag and I agreed we didn't have enough operators to sweep and catch all the growers, given the immense expanse of the canyon and the lack of perimeter coverage. The northern grow complex was too large and spread out, and at least a few of the squirrelly growers were likely to slip through our net. Fortunately, Spag offered a backup plan. With the sheriff's helicopter tied up flying high-altitude surveillance above us to relay critical radio traffic between our ground teams, Spag acquired additional air support for this type of contingency.

With a California Highway Patrol (CHP) helicopter on standby, we were ready to play our final card of the morning. Banking on the skill and confidence of our local CHP pilots, we would call them into the canyon for an aggressive, low-altitude sweep of the grow site, followed by suppressive and repetitive perimeter loops of the entire canyon below. Anyone working within the grow site below would either go to the ground and hide or, more likely, flee under the tree canopy via the connecting trail system in which we were concealed. We bet on the latter. Spag made the call.

Within minutes, the deafening roar of the CHP's Jet Ranger helicopter burst in low from the canyon bottom. I grinned as the helicopter's rotor wash pushed down the treetops, brush and grasses surrounding us on the ridgeline. Scripted perfectly, the pilot played to the geography of our site and brought the big ship in low from the west. Pinned down and easy to spot if they ran out the bottom of the canyon, the growers had only two ways to try to escape: straight uphill toward Rails and his team, or up and over the ridgeline trail straight to our team, now set up in ambush formation.

One minute later, under the roar of the Jet Ranger circling overhead, Miya, R.D. and I spotted the first movement on the trail. The man, running in a complete panic, didn't notice us just off the edge of the trail as he crested the ridge. He nearly ran into the flash hider on my M14's barrel. He got to know me better after that. I yelled at the grower to put up his hands and get on the ground. The grower froze in place, allowing R.D. a chance to handcuff him before he could run again.

Only 10 minutes later, we surprised another grower running the same frantic path as the first man. Just as before, it was too late for him when he reached us. The grower surrendered without a fight.

Spag's plan worked perfectly. The men, candid now that they were overwhelmed and defeated, told us three more accomplices worked the grow site below. When pressed, they were adamant that five growers ran the complex given its large size. They lost sight of their three partners when the chopper scattered them in all directions.

In the canyon below, Rails and his team pushed downhill into the grow site. After a careful yet unsuccessful sweep for the three outstanding suspects, the team secured and held the grow site, pending evidence collection and eradication. We instructed all teams to begin eradicating each site since it was already late in the morning. The temperatures climbed quickly. We had a long day of work ahead of us and we couldn't afford to spend any more time pursuing suspects.

Several patrol deputies positioned along exterior perimeter positions east of the northern grow site. We crossed our fingers in hopes our outside guys would get lucky. With the sheriff's helicopter doing sweeps along the outside perimeter toward Morgan Hill, and the CHP's Jet Ranger circling above Rails' team holding the grow below, we had a chance of intercepting these men on the run.

Still on top of the ridgeline above the Tohara northern and southern grows, Spag and I stood concealed in tree cover. Frustrated that three growers had gotten away during the helicopter sweep, we knew they couldn't be far away. Since the shifty growers didn't follow their partners into our trap to the south and wouldn't risk exposure farther west in the wide-open grasslands of the canyon bottom, we gambled that they moved uphill to the east. We focused our binoculars on that ridge. After all, if the roles were reversed, that's where we'd go.

Seconds later, an excited Spag tapped my arm and said, "I just saw them! Sneaky bastards are moving through the trees 400 yards out. They're double-timing it to the top."

"Crap, we don't have anyone up there. Let's go," I replied, as we sprinted along the ridgeline toward our target.

Spag fell in behind me, stride for stride, and radioed a SITREP for our air support and perimeter units to be ready. There was no way we were going to catch them from this far behind, but at least we could monitor their next move if they doubled back into the thick timber. Within minutes, we reached the spot where Spag first spotted the trio. Winded from a 400-yard sprint uphill over uneven terrain, and carrying our full kits and rifles, we gasped for breath and assessed.

Then saw them.

Just 100 yards above and camouflaged in earth-tone clothing, the trio climbed up on the edge of the road and looked down at us. We trained our weapons on the three and commanded them to surrender. The growers just smiled with no intention of giving up. They paused for a few seconds before disappearing over the edge of the road.

Frustrated and still filling my hungry lungs, I looked at Spag and shook my head in disgust. Spag just grinned and said, "Don't worry, buddy, we're not done yet. Let's move."

At the top of the mountain, we crested the edge of the road and scanned the area with our weapons. The growers were gone. Their tracks pointed east across the road and disappeared into the brush. Spag put out another SITREP on his radio, pressing the perimeter units to be ready for the growers to show up.

We walked along the ridgeline, looking for more tracks on the off chance the growers doubled back into the canyon. We found no sign of them and were about to hike back down to the southern grow site when some great news broke the radio silence. Two perimeter deputies spotted the trio walking down a dirt road toward Morgan Hill just minutes earlier. The three men told the deputies they were a landscaping crew walking to meet their boss for a pickup. With all three cut up and dirty from busting brush, the deputies laughed at their story and took them into custody.

Cartels often leave calling cards that help authorities tie them to crimes. This graffiti, found in a camp during the sweep of the second Tohara Canyon DTO complex, identifies the organizations behind the grow.

Spag didn't say a word. He held up his fist, meeting mine in midair as we quietly celebrated a complete victory. We caught all eight suspects working the three grow complexes. We felt elated at our success.

Rails' team cleared and assessed the Tohara north grow while Spag and I were chasing the last growers. The complex was clearly a cartel operation. It totaled more than 10,000 mature marijuana plants spread out over a quarter-mile on both sides of the canyon. An elaborate, well-camouflaged irrigation system and containers of banned poisons and pesticides supported the grow. Cartel graffiti found inside the tents and carved into manzanita trees throughout the site offered more clues. Gang names prolific throughout the complex, such as "La Familia," "Los Zetas" and "Antrax," identified affiliations with violent, well-established DTOs from the Michoacán region of central Mexico.

This is a graded and destroyed creek channel on the Sleepy Valley grow plot. It's what happens when water, already a scare resource, is redirected for illegal marijuana grows. Needless to say, the environmental consequences are significant.

Fortunately, our teams remained unharmed after discovering several tripwires, noise-makers and anti-personnel snares while sweeping trails. Rails' evidence collectors found various calibers of rifle and handgun ammunition, as well as a semi-automatic handgun in one of the tents, indicating the fleeing growers took guns with them to be ditched later. For the rest of the day, Rails and his teammates worked nonstop, bagging and tagging evidence, and eradicating the grow site.

Back on the southern Tohara site, Spag and I joined Miya, R.D., and Quinn to begin the arduous tasks of processing evidence, eradicating the grow and disabling the massive water pump and diversion dam at the bottom of the canyon. We spent several hours on these tasks, and by late afternoon, we called it a day.

At the Sleepy Valley grows, Hunter's team cataloged the numerous environmental crimes and damage on site. Besides the 10,000-plus plants the operators disposed of from the steep hillsides, they also addressed hundreds of pounds of hanging and drying budded marijuana. Like the other two grows, Hunter dealt with a massive streambed alteration and water diversion on the Sleepy Valley site, with that creek and its vegetation completely obliterated.

We needed to return to all three grow sites to conduct Natural Resource Damage Assessments (NRDA) with our CDFW biologists, but the heavy lifting of the operation was complete.

Exhausted, our entry teams returned just before sunset to the South Santa Clara County Sheriff's Substation to debrief the mission. Peeling off heavy armor kits and BDU tops in the parking lot, we relished the evening breeze, which quickly cooled our overheated bodies. This marked the most rewarding time of every mission: the relief, success and happiness that comes at the end of the operation. I said a short prayer, always grateful to see everyone safe back at base.

Totals for the day were an impressive eight DTO growers caught, 25,000 black market marijuana plants destroyed, eight long guns and a handgun seized, and six water-stealing and polluting diversions rectified.

The prisoner-holding area inside the substation was overloaded. I walked past J.R.'s crew, their heads hung down in defeat, and picked out the three runners Spag and I chased earlier. I stopped in mid-stride when I noticed their frowns as they looked up at me. Karma's a bitch, and it was my turn to smile.

However, the biggest fish, J.R. himself, remained outside of custody. We returned the following day to prepare for the final phase of the operation: taking down the ringleader once and for all.

ONE WEEK LATER – J.R.'S RESIDENCE – SOUTH SILICON VALLEY

For the first few days after the raids, J.R. lived in fear of being taken into custody, uncertain whether we had established crimes against him. He'd been careful to stay disconnected from the grow operations on the ranch, visiting them only a handful of times over the last four months. He never stepped foot on the property during the cultivation period and always covered his tracks, making sure he wasn't followed. By the fourth day, when we still hadn't come, J.R. must've breathed easy, feeling confident we had nothing on him.

That changed when a flash bang detonated at his front door one morning before dawn. Voices yelling, "Police! Search warrant! Demand entry!" snapped him to reality. We'd come for him after all.

Wisely, J.R. decided against a firefight. His rifles were locked in a gun safe in the bedroom. Only his .45-caliber Colt 1911 under the mattress offered any chance at fighting back. Without a complement of guards around the house as usual, he could not resist. He had no desire to die that day.

Hunter and a large complement of Sheriff's Emergency Response Team (SERT) operators flooded the large estate, detaining J.R. and his wife while searching the house. Spag, myself and several SERT operators cleared and searched an indoor grow operation within J.R.'s massive barn complex near the estate. Hunter's team executed our search warrant systematically within the residence, clearing every room of the large home. Large stacks of untraceable cash and numerous long guns were buried in the bedroom safe. We found paperwork helpful to our case in both buildings. Not surprisingly, we found more marijuana plants hidden within and growing throughout J.R.'s trees and landscaping around his home.

By mid-afternoon we completed all searches of the property and escorted J.R. to an idling squad car parked in his driveway. Waiting at the cruiser were Sheriff's Sergeant B.M. and Detective Dee — our jail-transport unit for the operation. They waited eagerly all morning for the tasks of taking J.R. back to jail. Hunter and I stood behind B.M. and Dee while they switched J.R.'s handcuffs, returning the entry team's pair before replacing them with their own. Dee directed J.R. to turn around and assume the arrest position before looking at me and Hunter and directing our attention to her belt.

"Do you think these will work?" Dee asked as she pulled a pair of bright-pink tactical handcuffs from her battle belt.

Hunter and I looked at each other and grinned before I replied quietly, "Very fitting, Dee. Tactical bling all the way."

Dee nodded and whispered, "This is for Debbie," before securing J.R.'s wrists in her colorful cuffs and placing him in the back seat of the squad.

Hunter and I watched in silence as the squad rolled down J.R.'s driveway. The excitement and relief on Hunter's face was evident. J.R.'s arrest marked the end of tactical operations on the ground — the most dangerous part of this case. Even with hundreds of hours of investigative and courtroom paperwork still ahead, we both breathed easy for the first time in weeks. The dangerous part of the operation was over.

Hunter turned to me and said, "Dee nailed it, Trailblazer. This one's for Debbie."

FALL 2013 – SAN JOSE SUPERIOR COURT – SILICON VALLEY

With charges of felony abetting and numerous environmental destruction crimes, J.R. pled guilty after more than two years of jury trial postponements. After serving a short stint in jail while awaiting trial, J.R. was released and placed on three years of felony probation, following his conviction.

Even though J.R.'s growers had no identification or carried falsified IDs, all eight men were accurately identified within days of apprehension. Typical of DTO operations, they were Mexican nationals in the United States illegally. Some had extensive violent criminal records and were charged with a multitude of cultivation felonies and environmental crime misdemeanors, qualifying them as deportable felons.

The NRDA reports generated by our biologists best described the environmental damage. Throughout the four grow complexes, fish and wildlife species had been decimated, and the diverted, polluted and obliterated streams within the Sleepy Valley and Tohara Canyon sites would need years to recover. Our experts calculated a conservative cost of $85,000 to restore the wildlife habitat and prevent any more loss and damage to the waterways connected to all four grow sites. Added to the penalty were the investigative costs and time that CDFW game wardens and biologists committed to the case. J.R. needed to pay $250,000 in restitution to our agency, while being bound legally to stop all un-permitted environmental disturbance work on his Sleepy Valley property.

As of this writing, no crimes have been detected on the property since the settlement five years ago. Although we're confident our efforts made a big enough dent to deter future violence and destruction in the area, we never dropped our guard. It's the least we can do, given Debbie's sacrifice and the integrity of our wildlife and water-quality resources. ✤

N37 05' 157"
W121 44' 729"

CHAPTER 02

MISSION CROY ROAD: GUNMEN, K9 PHEBE AND A PACK MULE NAMED STANLEY

"She is your friend, your partner, your defender, your dog. You are her life, her love, her leader. She will be yours, faithful and true, to the last beat of her heart. You owe it to her to be worthy of such devotion."

–Author Unknown

JUNE 2012 – CROY ROAD – SOUTH SANTA CLARA COUNTY

The marijuana grower struggled under the duress of Phebe's bite as our relentless K9 kept pressure on the man's right calf. Running full speed to catch up, Rumble and I could see this man was tough. Unlike other dangerous growers under a seasoned K9's control, this man did not scream.

Running just a few yards ahead of me, Rumble couldn't focus on Phebe or her suspect. His eyes locked on a second grower a few feet away. The second grower pulled out an automatic pistol from his waist, and my breath hitched. I couldn't get to the man fast enough. Everything around me moved in slow motion.

The next few seconds caused a change in the progression of our apprehension strategies for these dangerous men. Mission planning and tactics for our Marijuana Enforcement Team and other teams throughout the state would never be the same.

Three months earlier...

Teamed up with my sheriff's office MET partners, Spag and Hunter, on a cold, clear March day, we savored the perfect conditions for a recon scout. Also with us was the newest addition to our MET family, my 6-month-old K9 companion, Apollo. As my first dog since the passing of K9 Jordan a year and a half earlier, Apollo took to the woods instantly as a puppy. She seemed comfortable around operator teams and gunfire, after being exposed to both as a puppy.

Jordan's death still felt raw to all of us. My sheriff's office MET brothers took her loss as hard as I did. Losing a K9 partner is no different than losing a human operator. The pain and loss is devastating. Apollo's addition to our operational family helped to brighten everyone's day.

Apollo is an English Lab. She passed her companion obedience testing on her first attempt just a few days prior. Today would be her first time on a scout mission. It would test her focus, noise discipline and K9 fieldcraft in the woods.

Although March is unusually early for marijuana cultivators to begin planting in California, this site was an exception. With the start of the biggest drought in California's recent history, the light rains throughout Silicon Valley during the winter of 2011–12 catalyzed an early start of grow operations throughout the county. Area residents witnessed unusual vehicle traffic up and down Croy Road — a remote road surrounded by wooded hills a few miles west of rural Morgan Hill in southern Silicon Valley. Witnesses spotted small lights moving through the underbrush and tree canopy in the middle of the night on the vast wooded ridgeline on the south side of the road. This activity continued nightly for the past week.

Our scout team planned to access the suspected grow site from the west, far from the location of the suspected cultivation activity. We figured to hike to the top of the ridge and work along the edge of the eastern border of the grow site, approaching it from the west and above if possible. Tactical advantage

When it comes to combating illegal marijuana grows, nothing beats a great K9. K9 Phebe was every bit as brave and determined as her human counterparts. Here she is with MET operators after apprehending two armed suspects on the Croy Road Operation.

K9 Apollo during her first scout mission with Spag and Hunter. Dogs aren't just dogs in the field. They're partners.

would dictate our route once we reached the target area. Fortunately, we all knew the terrain well.

With Hunter on point and Spag following a few yards behind, Apollo and I fell in to the tail position as we ascended the ridge. The soft ground and wet brush made the climb virtually silent. The terrain throughout the county is usually much noisier and less forgiving later in the season. Apollo maintained her noise discipline and focus as she followed behind Spag at the end of her leash.

Approximately an hour after beginning our climb, Hunter spotted the first signs of a grow operation. Holding his AR-15 at the high-ready position, he whispered into his radio microphone, "We've got a brush wall 20 yards ahead at 10 o'clock."

Spag pivoted toward that position. I gave Apollo the hand signal to "hold." She sat down ahead of me, looking up to see what I would do next. I raised my POF AR-10 carbine and scanned the brush ahead through my Aimpoint Micro red-dot sight. I couldn't help the feeling of being watched. Concerned that a threat could move up behind us, I checked our back trail.

For the next few minutes, we remained frozen as I verified there were no threats beyond the brush wall with my pocket binoculars. When we resumed moving toward the wall, we saw that multiple coyote brush, chemise and manzanita branches had been freshly cut, interwoven and piled into a short boundary line. These brush-built boundary walls are common in grow operations all over California. Growers use them to not only enclose and disguise their cultivation sites, but to also make it difficult for law enforcement teams to penetrate them undetected. We all knew we were now on the edge of an active grow.

We paralleled the brush wall, looking for an unobstructed entry point into the area. Hunter found a good spot to cross the boundary 20 yards south of our original position. He tiptoed in first as Spag covered him with a rifle. I did the same for Spag. Spag turned to cover me as I un-tethered Apollo's leash before she slid through the brush wall. With Apollo at Spag's side, I moved across the boundary and fell into the tail gun position on our team once again.

A few seconds later, Hunter whispered into his mic, "Fresh digging and a shovel 10 yards ahead at 12 o'clock."

Again, Spag, Apollo and I froze as we scanned ahead. The shovel sported fresh dirt on its blade. It could've been used minutes ago, and we now knew there were growers in the perimeter ahead of us. Despite the fresh digging, we did not see any signs of marijuana plants in the ground. This crew was just getting started, preparing the ground and the irrigation system for planting.

Apollo turned her head, ears cocked forward, alert on something in the brush ahead of us. Sitting at my feet, she remained frozen and looking ahead. I scanned behind us once again as I heard Hunter in my ear mic say, "Two voices ahead, Spanish speaking, unknown distance, at our 10 o'clock." We stood dangerously close to the men running this grow.

The voices faded to silence. When Hunter felt confident the growers had left, he signaled us to move. Covering each other with our rifles once again, we retreated through the brush barrier one at a time. Now on point, I guided our team to some brushy cover well outside of the grow site perimeter. We took a long break and listened for movement behind us.

Over the next several months, we monitored this site to confirm plants in the ground before organizing one of our first allied-agency takedowns of 2012.

Following our scouting mission in March, we needed to conduct an aerial flyover of the site to verify plants in the ground. We had to solidly connect cultivation — and the multitude of other associated environmental crimes — to any suspects we encountered the day of the takedown. But with the sheriff's office helicopter down for multiple repairs, and my agency's air assets tied up on other details, we had no choice but to wait.

The sheriff's office helicopter was finally up and running the last week of May. Spag called me on a Friday afternoon, excited to share the good news about the bird. Since we only had the chopper for that Sunday afternoon, we jumped on the opportunity to fly. To avoid compromising the operation, Spag asked the pilot to make a single pass over the target site and to fly it from west to east — the same direction our scout team had hiked it more than a month earlier. Spag and I knew we needed to find plants quickly and get an accurate location once we did. If our GPS waypoints were marked even a few seconds too late, our coordinates could be a quarter-mile or more off target.

We flew south along the top of Loma Prieta, just a few hundred feet above the radio repeater towers, before banking east and making corrections toward the Croy Road ridgeline. Spag and I simultaneously smiled as we saw large marijuana plants below us. Rob could hear our excitement over the intercom as we articulated what we saw below. The grow site looked big. It stretched much farther to the east than we expected. Given the tree canopy and thick brush cover below, we knew we were likely seeing only a fraction of the plants on the ground. With the late afternoon sun setting slowly behind us, we continued east for some time before banking northwest and heading back.

After verifying the Croy Road site cultivation, we developed a plan. The location of the site made us concerned. The Uvas Creek watershed rested less than a mile down-canyon from the grow. With all of the site's drainages flowing into tributaries of Uvas Creek and Uvas Reservoir, we worried about the environmental impacts to water quality and sensitive wildlife species. With

The toxic chemicals at illegal grows spare no animal. This poisoned mountain lion was found in the Santa Cruz Mountains on a trespass grow site.

migrating steelhead and red-legged frogs (both threatened and/or endangered species) residing in those watersheds, we could only imagine the level of damage the grow site's fertilizers, pesticides and other poisons caused downstream.

We pulled together eight sheriff's deputies and six game wardens for an early June mission. Up front and on point with Hunter was our apprehension and arrest team's other long gunner, Miya, who is a sheriff's office sergeant, sniper and seasoned MET operator. In the constant effort to progress tactically and increase officer and suspect safety, we changed up tactics. Until now, we utilized light runners (lightly armed and equipped apprehension specialists) behind our two riflemen on point to pursue and capture unarmed suspects. That day, however, we added a specialized apprehension K9 to do the job.

Positioned right behind Miya in our entry team were Rumble — who personifies the term "mountain man," having grown up in the dense forests of

Booby traps present one of the most dangerous, and indiscriminate threats for MET teams and the public. Imagine a family spending quality time in the outdoors together stumbling into this punji pit. It could've happened. This booby trap was found in a national park.

northern California and Idaho — and his legendary dual-purpose K9, Phebe. Phebe, a Belgian Malinois, was one of the most highly skilled and versatile dogs in the CDFW's K9 program. Because of the violent nature of the growers we encounter, any tactical advantage is critical. An apprehension K9 skilled in working remote, wooded grow sites is rare and invaluable.

The day's operation didn't mark the first time I worked with the pair. During the 2011 season, while our agency was filming *Wild Justice* (the first game warden reality show on the National Geographic channel), I teamed up with Rumble and Phebe to integrate them into our DTO cultivation operations in the Silicon Valley. Beyond the positive outreach the show generated for our entire agency, I was excited to work together. Their stellar reputations preceded them.

As Rumble's support and cover, I was positioned behind him. Behind me was Quell, a new team member from the sheriff's office and a Marine with multiple tours in Iraq. Harp, a Coast Guard Spec Ops veteran and seasoned deputy, took up the tail gunner position.

Spag and my warden partner, Markos, served as the point men on our secondary team, the Quick Reaction Force (QRF), following 25 yards behind our apprehension team. Behind Markos on the QRF were sheriff's office operators Raptor, Fleck and Berric — all seasoned tactical officers. Backing them up, and strategically positioned below the grow site and not far above Croy Road was our perimeter team, headed up by wardens Quinn and Bones. They were tasked with catching any fleeing suspects.

Hundreds of feet above and a half-mile west of our perimeter team, our entry team hiked up the ridge, below and west of the grow site. The dry, crunchy leaf litter and grass made it almost impossible to remain silent as we ascended. Deliberate foot placement, combined with smooth upper body movement, kept us nearly invisible as we closed the distance to the complex.

After covering the final 100 yards, Hunter stopped the team. The trail we used to enter the complex had been completely altered. Dry manzanita branches covered the entrance and scattered across the footpath. This noisy trail trap would, at best, spook the growers when we entered, and at worst, allow them to ambush us. However, unlike in 2005 when Mojo was shot and almost killed after our team moved through a similar noisy brush tunnel, we were much more prepared now.

As usual, I carried only my handgun, TASER, arrest tools and a light pack to support Rumble and Phebe. I also packed a small brush clipper to deal with this exact obstacle. Hunter called me forward to cut a trail through the labyrinth of brush ahead. Miya and Hunter covered me with their AR-15s as I moved to the front.

Dropping to my knees, I kept an eye out for booby traps while clipping brush and branches. In slow motion, I moved each freshly cut branch to the side of the trail. Now on point, with Miya and Hunter covering me, I crawled through the brush, unsure if any threats waited on the other side. My heart raced as I

This revolver was seized from one of the DTO growers apprehended during the Croy Road Operation. Between the gunfights and the booby traps, comparisons to a war zone are on the mark. It's an unfortunate reality for public lands in California and elsewhere in the United States.

This should be the scene of an idyllic trout stream. Instead, it's polluted with camp waste.

cut away the obstruction. With my handgun trained ahead, I pushed forward another 10 feet and froze. Directly ahead, and as far down the hillside as I could see, stood thousands of large marijuana plants.

We knew the growers could walk down the trail at any moment. We waited another five minutes, looking and listening for movement around us. Seeing and hearing nothing, Hunter signaled the team to move farther down the trail into the grow site.

Contact with the growers seemed imminent. With the main trail in the middle of a downhill slope, we positioned ourselves at a choke point to ambush the growers when they worked up the ridge to water their crop. Our other

These are some of the deadly pesticides and poisons used at the Croy Road grow site. It takes only a tablespoon of Furadan to kill aquatic wildlife for miles.

advantage was the K9. Phebe's keen sense of smell could detect approaching suspects well before they saw us.

Our timing was perfect. Within five minutes of setting up on our hilly vantage point, Rumble and I spotted two growers emerging from the bottom of the grow site. Both were dressed in olive drab military camouflage, quietly speaking in Spanish. We were alarmed to see a stainless steel pistol on the right hip of one of the men. Rumble whispered into the radio, "Two suspects at 12 o'clock, 25 yards out, headed toward us. Be advised, one has a handgun on his right hip."

Given the gun violence we experienced from growers in the past, and after several brutal assaults on Phebe during similar apprehension missions, we weren't taking any chances. The apprehension needed to be as surprising as possible. When the growers were approximately 20 yards out, Rumble gave Phebe the apprehension command. He released her from the leash and whispered over the radio, "Dog's away!"

Phebe shot toward the men as Rumble and I sprinted behind her. Rushing forward with our pistols trained on the men, we yelled, "Police! Put your hands up and don't move!"

Approximately an hour after beginning our climb, Hunter spotted the first signs of a grow operation. Holding his AR-15 at the high-ready position, he whispered into his radio microphone, "We've got a brush wall 20 yards ahead at 10 o'clock."

The growers stopped just in time to see our speedy K9 closing in. With their eyes as wide as silver dollars and their mouths open in shock, the men didn't see us closing in behind Phebe until it was too late. Before they could run, Phebe tackled the man on the right, bit his right calf and forced him to the ground. The grower with the pistol, seeing us closing in, reached for his holstered pistol. In a split-second decision, Rumble and I switched roles. Rumble yelled to me, "Take my dog!" and ran past Phebe and her struggling grower.

I now had to handle Phebe and her suspect, while Rumble worked to keep the armed gunman from harming our team. Phebe's captured grower struggled and kicked.

Rumble, now face to face with his gunman a few yards ahead, trained his Glock on the suspect's chest. The man hesitated a moment before releasing the grip on his pistol and putting his hands up.

With Miya and Hunter covering, Rumble placed the man in handcuffs and removed a loaded revolver.

Meanwhile, I couldn't get to my suspect fast enough. Thankfully, Phebe's bite slowed him down. She made it difficult for him to aim the pistol, affording me the opportunity to close the gap and take control. I jumped on the suspect's back as Phebe continued to keep pressure on his calf. I struck the gunman between the shoulder blades, yelling at him to drop the pistol. Then I grabbed both of his hands and placed them in handcuffs.

Now that the gunman was no longer a threat, I needed to call Phebe off her bite. Rumble trained all of us to handle her in the event he was injured or tied up on another threat. I heard Spag behind me moving the QRF up to support us with a perimeter around our two suspects. I knew Spag's concern. We only cleared a small part of the grow complex and had not even found a kitchen or camp yet. More armed growers could be in the area, along with booby traps and toxic chemicals.

Following a quick pat-down of the suspect's pockets and waistband, I picked up the handgun, a World War II-era semi-automatic .32-caliber Russian Tokarev pistol, from the ground and unloaded it. I showed it to Harp.

"That was close, lieutenant," he said. "And that round was intended for us."

I let out a sigh before responding, "Way too close, brother! And God bless Phebe. She saved us from another gunfight today."

With the scene secure, our team divided up to tackle the rest of the grow site. Rumble, Phebe, Miya, Hunter and Quell hiked out and cleared the complex. Spag cleaned and dressed the gunman's wound before sitting him down in the shade under a small tree. The gunman still had to be walked out of the grow site, medically treated and cleared at the hospital later that day.

Within 30 minutes, Hunter's team found the growers' camp, their kitchen, the marijuana-processing area and multiple check dams and water diversions. Like all these complexes, the grow site was a mess. With several tons of camp trash, human and cooking waste, fertilizers, pesticides and thousands of feet of black plastic irrigation hose littering the ground, we had our work cut out for us.

The two growers turned out to be the only men on the grow site at that time. With the harvest a few weeks away, the men didn't yet need additional workers on site. Although most of the marijuana budded, none of it was quite ready to be harvested.

Next up came time to process, eradicate and environmentally restore the site. Hunter and his men found several containers of Furadan — a highly toxic pesticide banned in the United States — within the site. We realized the growers likely used this poison throughout the site's watering system. A mere tablespoon of this substance was enough to decimate all the fish and other aquatic wildlife for miles in Croy Creek. As such, we donned nitrile gloves to protect us from the numerous poisons in the area.

In the field, it's important to adapt to conditions. Sometimes that means commissioning a pack mule to haul away marijuana at a remote grow site.

With the team code 4 and the eradication phase underway, Fleck relieved me from guarding Phebe's gunman so I could SITREP my command staff. I walked another 20 yards up the ridge away from the prisoner to use my cell phone. As I gave an update about the K9 bite apprehension, Fleck interrupted and yelled, "Rumble, L.T., come here quick! Check Phebe out!"

I ran down the hill. Phebe sat with her face just inches from the apprehended grower. She stared him down as if to say, "I'm watching and will drop you again if you try to harm my team."

Rumble burst through the brush from below us and yelled, "Phebe, get over here!" He pulled her back from the suspect. Embarrassed, Rumble apologized. The Fur Missile, as we called Phebe, had slipped out of her tether and snuck over to send a message to our suspect when her master wasn't looking.

Still, we had a problem. Without helicopter support, we needed to remove everything by hand. None of us looked forward to removing the plants. Obstacles like this are common to MET operations, which is why the ability to adapt is a necessity. Our MET motto is "fill and flow," and I lived it that day. Fortunately, my friend John lived nearby. John runs pack mules in the

Hunter and his men found several containers of Furadan — a highly toxic pesticide banned in the United States — within the site. We realized the growers likely used this poison throughout the site's watering system. A mere tablespoon of this substance was enough to decimate all the fish and other aquatic wildlife for miles in Croy Creek.

Sierra Nevadas during the summer. We were relieved to learn that he had one seasoned mule, Stanley, left on his ranch. Stanley was a seasoned and trail-savvy black mule. We couldn't help but laugh at the novelty.

For the next two hours, we cut and stacked massive bundles of budded marijuana plants on Stanley's packboard before walking him down to the transport trucks. Even with Stanley's help, many of us carried bundles to expedite the 7,000-plant extradition. We finished in mid-afternoon, but not before restoring the water diversions and gathering debris for removal by helicopter later.

Our team walked single-file down the ridge to some much-needed cold drinks in our trucks below. I pondered the tactics we needed to push on the MET K9 front while I hiked down the canyon. We proved why we needed these progressive tactics to keep us safe and effective against dangerous criminals. It wasn't only for our own sakes, but also for the environment and the public. ✹

N 36° 59' 779"
W 121° 40' 631"

CHAPTER 03

GUNFIGHT ON BODFISH CREEK: ALONE AND OUTGUNNED

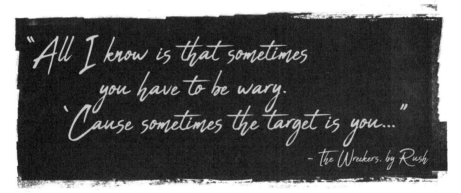

"All I know is that sometimes you have to be wary. 'Cause sometimes the target is you..."

— the Wreckers, by Rush

JUNE 28, 2012 – BODFISH CREEK – SANTA CRUZ MOUNTAINS

Fausto and Jave were proud of this *mota* complex — their first solo operation in California — and grateful their cartel boss trusted them enough to run it. Although they hadn't known each other long, Fausto and Jave enjoyed working together. They had a lot in common; both were ambitious, close in age and hailed from the same region in Mexico. Trained by the best growers in Michoacán, they proved quick learners and experts in locating water, even during drought years. The pair never lost a grow to law enforcement in either Mexico or California.

Although their template for success included remaining undetected throughout each grow season, they were armed with semi-automatic rifles, and longed for a fight. A fight to defend the grow would solidify their trust within their organization, and the *caballero* in each of them fantasized about going *mano a mano* with invaders.

The Bodfish Creek DTO complex's dense growth of marijuana plants.

Soon, they would get their chance.

As he had every morning for the last two months, Fausto assessed the camp at first light, scanning for intruders or anything out of the ordinary. He knew from his training this was the witching hour — the time when law enforcement operatives liked to execute raids. This morning, for now, all remained quiet.

Fausto roused Jave. Although chilly now, the day would heat up into the 90s, and the growers needed to get the entire 5,000-plant grow site watered before breakfast. They headed out.

Separated from Fausto by 5-foot-tall marijuana plants, Jave walked to the end of each row. He opened the valve allowing water from the main line to charge each row's smaller, pressurized waterline, leading to drip emitters at the base of each plant. The men spent weeks building this irrigation system throughout the complex. A half-mile away, through dense forest, brush and rock, their main water source, a tributary to Bodfish Creek, provided plenty for their crop. Nearly 3,000 feet of camouflaged, 1-inch black poly pipe lay hidden on and under the ground.

Jave irrigated plants while Fausto checked the edges of the complex for animal and rodent damage. The d-CON rat poison, and especially the "*el Diablo*" poison their boss provided did a fine job of killing every insect, bird and mammal it touched.

Fausto's attention turned to a breaking branch uphill of the grow site. He listened intently, his rifle pointed toward the sound. Noise-making obstructions lined the trail as an early warning system. His heart must've skipped a beat when he realized someone was coming.

Fausto spotted Jave. They'd both heard the movement above.

Without a word, Fausto signaled his partner to follow. The growers glided past their camp to the bottom edge of the complex. Facing a short wall of downed trees and brush, Fausto slung his rifle over his shoulder and moved a small, pre-cut manzanita bush within the wall, exposing one of their many carefully hidden escape trails. With Jave covering their back trail, the men slipped through the wall, replacing the bush behind them.

The men moved toward the intruders to set up and wait them out. Stealth and familiarity would allow them to pick off the intruders one by one. Finally, they had a chance to make their boss proud.

One month earlier ...

When I saw Hunter was calling, I picked up my cell phone right away. He told me our allied-agency partners from the Santa Cruz County Sheriff's Office spotted a grow site on our side of the county line during a helicopter overflight. We had coordinates to follow up on.

This one was in an area where we had never had DTO cultivation activity before: southwestern Santa Clara County in the southern end of the Santa Cruz Mountains. The site was tucked behind locked gates in dense, redwood-covered mountains above Bodfish Creek. The grow was about 3 miles south of Hecker Pass (Highway 152) in no man's land. Only one timber company dirt road accessed and paralleled the ridgeline to the south of Hecker Pass. This place gave me a sense of nostalgia. I had a long personal and professional history with the area. I'd caught my first trout under my father's guidance more than 35 years earlier in nearby Sprig Lake, a natural trout fishery right near Bodfish Creek. Coincidentally, Hunter, also a Santa Clara County native, caught trout out of Sprig Lake in his youth as well.

The environmental sensitivity of the region caused us great concern. Steelhead spawn in Bodfish Creek each year. The fish swim a long distance from the Pacific Ocean to the clean gravel beds of the Bodfish to lay their eggs. Steelhead are a threatened species in California. Their numbers decline each year from water-quality degradation, pollution, erosion and widespread turbidity on their spawning beds. Hunter and I felt the need to protect these fish, especially from the devastating effects of a marijuana-growing operation.

At dawn, I met up with Hunter, Spag and Riz (a seasoned sheriff's deputy who assisted us on MET operations). We convoyed in two patrol vehicles to a locked gate on Hecker Pass Highway that opened access onto the ridgeline road and the suspected grow area. To avoid compromising the site, we didn't drive past the gate. Instead, we walked down the road, careful to leave no tracks. We preferred this quiet, deliberate scouting method.

Stalking into a suspected grow site from a long distance has advantages over a short hike. Besides getting a good workout, hiking keeps our fieldcraft skills sharp and makes us more aware of our surroundings. Knowing when bird and other animal activity happens and how it sounds in an area, for example, can be helpful. Once we're familiar with a targeted area, anything out of the ordinary stands out as an indicator that we are close to a grow complex or the growers working within. As my hunting and fieldcraft mentors had always told me, becoming one with the wilderness is more than invigorating and beautiful, it's an awareness that can mean the difference between life and death.

With Hunter on point, Spag covered our six in the tail gunner position, while Riz and I took up the middle. Grass and brush choked the dirt road behind the gate. The faint tracks indicated vehicles seldom traveled there. The dry ground, with a thin layer of soft dirt over the top, made man tracks easy to see. However, after almost 3 miles we didn't spot anything suspicious.

Jave irrigated plants while Fausto checked the edges of the complex for animal and rodent damage. The d-CON rat poison, and especially the *"el Diablo"* poison their boss provided did a fine job of killing every insect, bird and mammal it touched.

Frustrated, we moved off the trail and took a knee, concealed behind a brush line. We knew our suspects must use this road for *something*. Something wasn't adding up.

Perhaps the growers disguised their tracks. Growers sometimes cover the bottom of their shoes with felt to avoid leaving tracks. Some clever growers even made stilts that left imprints in the shape of cattle hooves. The coordinates from our helicopter crew put the grow on the ridgeline directly above us and to the west less than a quarter-mile, so an uphill trail or some other grow site clues should have been visible. We combed the area multiple times and still found nothing.

We agreed the coordinates given to us from the Santa Cruz helicopter crew were likely inaccurate. It wouldn't be the first time. Locking in accurate GPS coordinates from high above a grow site in a fast-moving chopper is difficult. Knowing the grow could be anywhere in a mile-wide perimeter, we focused to the east and downhill from the road on our hike back to the trucks.

Our luck changed about halfway back to the gate. While checking the downhill side of the road, we noticed a creek drainage that flowed under the road and downhill through culverts toward Bodfish Creek. Knowing where there's water, there's likely a grow, we stopped and assessed the drainage. This drainage was geographically perfect for a DTO grower's gravity-fed poly pipe irrigation system. We heard the faint sound of water flowing downhill of the road, but saw nothing suspicious.

Finally, Riz hit pay dirt when he noticed something out of place in the culvert drainage approximately 30 feet below the road. Small limbs and brush cuttings covered half-gallon-jug-sized rocks, spread on the ground in a line below us. There are no straight lines in nature.

Hunter took a knee and covered the downhill side of the road with his AR-15 as Spag and I covered all other fields of fire in a tight 360-degree perimeter with our rifles. Once our perimeter was set, Riz scaled down the steep hillside into the drainage. He turned over each rock slowly, examining the silty ground underneath. Sure enough, under the second rock rested the partially exposed edge of a one-inch-diameter black poly pipe, buried in the dirt. Riz dug around the pipe to expose the full circumference of an un-faded, new waterline. He shook it up and down, feeling for the weight of water inside. He looked up at us and nodded, confirming the line was charged with flowing water.

The discovery confirmed two facts. First, we could follow the active irrigation line to our target DTO grow site somewhere in the redwood forest below. Second, and just as important, this waterline stole much-needed water from the dwindling steelhead fishery in Bodfish Creek.

JUNE 28, 2012 – DIRT LOGGING ROAD – SANTA CRUZ MOUNTAINS

Two weeks later, our allied-agency MET assembled around patrol vehicles on the dirt road off Hecker Pass Highway. To minimize noise, we parked our patrol vehicles behind the access gate a mile from the waterline drainage, preferring to stalk in and catch the growers by surprise.

To our disappointment, Rumble and Phebe were tied up on another DTO cultivation operation in Shasta County. As a result, we decided to use light runners to handle any physical apprehensions, the old school way. This light-runner tactic increased officer risk and wouldn't be nearly as effective as using a seasoned K9 like Phebe.

After a final weapons and comms check, our stack hiked down the road toward our target. Hunter was our eyes and ears up front. Spag followed him, positioned to protect the light runners in the event things "got western" during a suspect chase and apprehension. ACOGs (4X Trijicon Advanced Combat Optical Gunsights) adorned their rifles for better visibility and accuracy in the densely wooded, low-light conditions.

Markos and I served as light runners. We equipped with light packs, our Glock .40-caliber handguns and TASERs. This made us faster and able to go hands-on with combative suspects much easier. This also meant it was Markos' first mission in which he left his recently issued Patriot Ordnance Factory P308 Edge carbine in the truck. The rifle was new, versatile and equipped to handle any threat (man or large animal) in a wilderness MET operation. Understandably, Markos had reservations when leaving his new carbine behind.

Behind me and Markos was Harp — the operator from the sheriff's office

DTO growers haul supplies while wearing felt shoe covers. These devices help cover tracks, especially on dirt roads.

A pair of handmade wooden cattle hoof stilts. Trespass growers use counter-tracking devices like these to disguise their tracks in areas where cattle are present.

who covered me when Phebe saved us from a gunfight on the Croy Road mission. He brought along his AR-15 again for the day's mission. Behind Harp were his sheriff's office partners, Quell and Berric, followed by my two young warden squad mates, Quinn and Jerry, who carried their new POF carbines on the day's operation — their first since the Croy Road takedown earlier that month.

We made quick time down the road to our jump-off point in the pre-dawn darkness. The chilly air cooled us down from the hot and heavy plate carrier, backpack, weapon and ammunition kits we carried. Just before sunrise, Hunter stopped us and took a knee in some tall grass just off the road. He eyed the waterline drainage 50 yards ahead for activity. Convinced no growers were on or near the waterline, we moved up.

Hunter descended over the edge of the road, with Spag covering. Spag followed his tracks down the embankment, with the rest of us following in order, each covering the man in front as he dropped into the drainage. Within a minute, all nine of us slithered down the embankment and were now back in a tight stack on the barely visible waterline trail. With sunrise imminent and the woods waking up around us, we started the stalk.

For the next hour, slower was better. Dry leaves covered the waterline trail, making it noisy to step on. The forest around Bodfish Creek was different from the scrub oak and manzanita-choked terrain we usually operated in. The jungle-like terrain filled with large redwoods, giant ferns and lush vegetation proved difficult to maneuver through.

A mile down the canyon, Hunter stopped our team and scanned the sparse trail ahead. The waterline disappeared under a large patch of manzanita and coyote brush, with the trail diverting away from the waterline to the north. After a few minutes of listening and letting the woods settle, we moved around the brush patch. We saw the first signs of our target within a few steps of clearing the vegetation: thousands of marijuana plants. We were on the downhill side of a large grow, and the trail ahead looked much more defined. Knowing the men running this complex were likely close, we paired up in concealed, defensible positions along the trail and listened again for grower activity. The distinct hissing sound of water spraying out of irrigation lines broke the morning silence.

Seeing no sign of movement, we eased into the grow site and stopped inside its edge. We glided from our ranger file stack into an online formation. One operator peeled right, with the next moving left, and so on until our entire team was side by side, approximately 3 to 5 yards apart in a skirmish line spanning more than 50 yards. This allowed us to sweep a dense grow site without missing essential elements (suspects, firearms, booby traps, trails, grow poisons, etc.). The line formation also eliminated a cross-fire situation.

The marijuana plants were so large and healthy that we couldn't see our feet below the thick cannabis canopy as we followed the trail system. I noticed that all of the plants on the downhill side of the grow where we entered had been watered before we arrived. The plants from the middle of the grow site uphill to its termination, however, were bone dry — a sign the growers had hastily abandoned their morning watering ritual. My heart sank. The growers must have seen or heard us and slipped out of the complex.

Harp radioed that he and Quell found the complex's camp and kitchen. They discovered a still-warm pot of water on a propane stove and a ready-to-cook meal on a table. This confirmed my suspicions that we bumped the growers during our entry.

Within 10 minutes, we cleared the entire grow, camp and kitchen area

If you come across a makeshift kitchen in the woods, you're probably not in the presence of ordinary campers. This is the DTO grower kitchen within the Bodfish Creek grow complex.

and held a wide 360-degree perimeter using the best cover around us. We assessed our options. We agreed we'd been detected, but we could not know for sure. I remembered something my friend and special operations covert team leader, Alpha, used to say when we thought we were compromised on undercover operations: "You're not burned, until you're burned." We were not going to give up. We decided to wait out our targets and surprise them upon their return.

The environmental sensitivity of the region caused us great concern. Steelhead spawn in Bodfish Creek each year ... Their numbers decline each year from water-quality degradation, pollution, erosion and widespread turbidity on their spawning beds. Hunter and I felt the need to protect these fish, especially from the devastating effects of a marijuana-growing operation.

With no large trees to provide hard cover, Markos and I set up in the shade on the lower edge of the grow site, 25 yards outside of the camp. Completely surrounded by marijuana plants, we were concealed just off the main trail. Jerry positioned himself slightly above and behind us, ready to provide support with his powerful .308-caliber carbine. The rest of the team spread out to complete the perimeter.

After an hour of silence and anticipation, we heard movement outside of the grow complex. We heard intermittent crunching and the sound of branches breaking underfoot coming from the direction of Bodfish Creek. I cupped my hands behind my ears and listened. Were we hearing growers coming back to check on their complex, or were we hearing them moving away from us to escape? Were the sounds even human? Whatever the source, it moved deliberately before falling silent. When the sounds resumed, they were slow and faint, never lasting more than a minute or two.

For the next two hours, the same sound pattern repeated itself another half-dozen times. The steep canyon below engendered surreal acoustics and made the sounds fluctuate from loud to quiet and back to loud again, echoing up the mountain to our position. Like someone adjusting a volume knob on a stereo, the echo made it even more difficult to calculate origin and distance. The movement now sounded like men stalking toward our position.

We were being hunted.

We maintained weapon readiness and waited to see what unfolded.

Besides the likelihood of several armed growers closing in on us, my thoughts also traveled to another problem. My patrol captain, "D.N.," had ordered me to attend an allied-agency watershed meeting that afternoon, much to my frustration. The timing couldn't be worse. At 11 a.m. I would need to hike back up to my patrol truck. I'd be doing so alone, without cover, and leaving Markos unsupported as a light runner. Regardless, I would never be insubordinate, and I prayed we would catch suspects early in the mission.

Looking at my watch, I saw the deadline was a few minutes away. Sick to my stomach at the thought of leaving my brothers before the site was secure, I signaled to Markos and Jerry that it was time for me to go and radioed the rest of our team with the same message. I hated putting them in this position.

I found myself back on the western edge of the grow site after 10 minutes and took a knee, concealing myself in the shadows of some coyote brush. I needed to listen and assess. We have a team rule that no one explores a trail or travels alone into un-cleared territory, and I reluctantly broke this rule against my better judgment.

Suddenly, I heard footsteps. They were louder than before. They repeated the same pattern as earlier, but without the echo factor of the steep canyon, the sounds were more defined and easier to assess. They were clearly getting closer.

Alone and armed with only my pistol, I cursed myself. The sounds weren't more than 25 yards away now. This had to be the worst tactical situation of my career.

The footsteps continued for the next five minutes, getting fainter as they headed toward the grow site. Now safe for me to break silence, I needed to warn my brothers of the incoming threat. I slowed my breathing before whispering the SITREP into my radio mic. Spag acknowledged, and I resumed my hike up the waterline trail. Eager to make it to the road and my patrol truck undetected, I moved quickly, taking short breaks to listen for more movement, but I didn't hear any. Within an hour, I raced down the pavement of Hecker Pass Highway toward Silicon Valley in my truck to make D.N.'s meeting on time.

A camouflaged grower tent within the Bodfish Creek complex.

Fausto and Jave stood motionless in the shade of three large redwood trees. Since bailing out on their escape trail, the growers backtracked east toward their camp. In more than three hours, neither grower had detected any signs of intruders. No helicopters flew overhead, and no wardens or cops had descended into their grow.

The pair navigated through the dense brush and into their camp. Seeing no fresh sign of compromise, the men picked their way toward the sunlit grow site.

Markos kneeled, his .40-caliber Glock 22 at the low ready, with his eyes locked on the camp's exit trail. Knowing Jerry covered close behind with his big carbine was a relief, but the long silence around camp alarmed him. The woods were too quiet. Markos' instincts and years of experience screamed the growers were close.

What had been a well-concealed, shaded ambush point earlier was now illuminated by bright sunlight. Any movement could get a teammate killed. Sitting statue-still amongst the marijuana plants, Markos put his trust in his camouflage. Suddenly a rifle barrel emerged from the shadows along the trail. The grower stepped out next, carrying a knife on his hip, just 25 yards away. Markos brought his Glock up to the high ready in anticipation. That's when he noticed a second grower sporting a long gun. Markos knew he needed to make a move fast before he was spotted.

Laying as small and concealed as possible against the ground, Markos locked his front sight on the lead grower's chest and yelled, "Police! Drop your weapons and don't move!"

Startled, the lead gunman pivoted his body and rifle toward the command. Markos fired two shots in rapid succession. The sledgehammer of two 180-grain, .40-caliber bullets hit Fausto's lower torso and right arm. Fausto dropped his rifle and fell backwards, hitting Jave in the chest. Both men went to the ground, breaking Jave's rifle stock in half during the fall. Although Jerry was right behind Markos, his position did not afford a safe angle to engage — an unfortunate, but not uncommon, situation for this type of dense terrain.

Fausto crawled back into the shadows of the camp and gave Jave the bail-out signal. They slipped down their escape trail, moving away from the complex as fast as possible. From the overwatch position above the camp, Harp engaged the moving threats with his AR-15, but the thick timber and vegetation absorbed the shots.

Markos radioed out a SITREP for the team, confirming two armed suspects on the run. The team stayed paired up and held a perimeter against any threats to follow. We needed to preserve everything within and around the camp because the whole complex had become a crime scene. The officer-involved shooting (OIS) investigation would follow that afternoon.

I was at home changing uniforms for my meeting when my cell phone rang.

An aerial view of the 5,000-plant Bodfish Creek grow complex. Bodfish Creek is a migration and spawning channel for threatened steelhead.

Markos clears a DTO grower camp in the Silicon Valley foothills.

It was our dispatch center, and I already knew the message: our team had just been in a gunfight. My heart sank when I learned Markos was the only shooter from our agency. I felt horrible for leaving my teammates behind, and even worse for not being in the fight when it got dangerous for Markos. Thankfully, he came out of the conflict unscathed, but I was still furious.

I took a deep breath before calling D.N. As professionally as I could, I told him I was headed back to support my team. D.N. stammered and agreed, adding that he was also headed that way. I hammered the gas pedal to the floor in my truck as anger swelled. D.N.'s directive could have cost officer lives; this must not happen again.

The growers made it to the bottom of the ridge below the grow site, concealed in a large fern garden along the edge of Bodfish Creek. With significant blood loss, Fausto was done running. He told Jave he was going to bleed out and die if he didn't turn himself in. The two men discussed a new plan, and Fausto gave Jave a minute's head start before making the worst call of his life.

I met up with Miya at the jump-off point to the grow site. To my pleasant surprise, I also linked up with Snake and Apache, my long-time sheriff's office MET partners from 2005 to 2009. From the trailhead, we descended into the complex, moving quickly to reach our team. I wanted Markos to receive the support he needed. This was the first time he'd pulled the trigger, and that changed the situation significantly.

As we moved, a bizarre dispatch call came in over our radios. The wounded grower Markos had engaged had just called 911 on his cell phone. He reported being shot by the police and requested medical assistance. He was willing to turn himself in as long as he was not shot at or assaulted by law enforcement officers.

He hunted us after we penetrated his illegal and environmentally devastating marijuana grow, but now he claimed to be a victim? Go figure!

Fausto turned himself in within the next hour. He was picked up from inside a rancher's barn near Bodfish Creek, eager for relief for his gunshot wounds.

After reaching the complex, I found Markos sitting with Jerry and Quinn near the grower camp. Quinn was calm, but Jerry looked worried and pulled me aside. He apologized for being unable to cover Markos with rifle fire when the growers showed up. I assured him that these ops are never predictable, and the terrain rarely presented good positioning. I reminded him that no matter how well we prepare for a mission, or what tactics we use, the risks are never fully alleviated. The danger is ever present.

Markos seemed calm and collected, but I could tell he was shaken. As agency supervisor and team leader on scene, I needed to see that he was supported and not questioned about the incident at that early point in the investigation. More importantly, as his longtime warden partner and friend, I wanted to make sure he was all right.

Miya, Snake, Apache and several other team members from the sheriff's office preserved the site for OIS investigators arriving later. Those of us involved in the early morning mission hiked out of the site. We spoke few words on the climb up to our patrol trucks. Markos rode with me to the Incident Command (IC) center set up in Mt. Madonna County Park at the top of Hecker Pass Highway. The one-on-one time in my truck calmed both of us and gave Markos time to prepare for the impending OIS investigation. Everyone involved would be interviewed over the next several hours. As one of two shooters from our team, Markos would be interviewed last, making his day the longest.

D.N. waited for us with an embarrassed look when we reached the IC. We would never again speak of his decision to pull me from the mission for a meeting. D.N. redeemed himself with support throughout the OIS-investigation process.

Per protocol, I collected Markos' Glock as evidence for the post-incident investigation and replaced it with a spare pistol from HQ before we drove to the San Jose Sheriff's Office headquarters for interviews. Like our previous OIS investigations, our thorough interviews ran late into the night. Everyone was smoked when we were done. Twenty straight hours had passed since our early morning briefing.

Four days later, Spag and I assembled a team to go back into the grow site to complete the eradication and reclamation phases of our mission. We eradicated 5,000 marijuana plants and removed more than a mile of black poly pipe irrigation line. We also collected a ton of grow complex fertilizers, pesticides, other poisons and waste. It felt great knowing the water diversions into Bodfish Creek were removed and the full flow of the sensitive waterway restored for the benefit of steelhead and all other wildlife downstream.

Although Jave was still on the run, Fausto was out of surgery and recovering from his gunshot wounds. He remained in custody at our San Jose main littering within 150 feet of a state waterway and water pollution. Fausto faced up to 15 years in prison.

After several pre-trial delays, Fausto pleaded guilty three months later to most of the charges, saving us from a lengthy jury trial. He received five years in prison. We were pleased with the sentence, given he was convicted not only for the cultivation, assault, and firearms use charges, but also for many environmental crimes.

Jave, unfortunately, was still at large.

The OIS investigation concluded that Markos and Harp were justified in their use of deadly force. This finding, coupled with Fausto's conviction, put closure to the incident for all of us. With so much at stake for Markos and Harp, they felt especially relieved.

For his bravery, decisiveness and sacrifice while protecting his teammates from harm during the Bodfish Creek Mission, the agency awarded Markos its highest honor: the Medal of Valor. Jerry, Quinn, and I were also awarded our agency's Distinguished Service Medal for bravery, decisiveness and teamwork throughout the dangerous incident. I was incredibly proud of Markos for his courage and actions when fending off two gunmen intent on doing us harm. I was also extremely proud of Jerry and Quinn for performing so bravely and decisively on such a high-risk mission so early in their careers. ✺

N 36 00' 082"
W 118 13' 678"

CHAPTER 04

CDFW'S MET: AMERICA'S FIRST CONSERVATION OFFICER SPECIAL OPERATIONS MARIJUANA ENFORCEMENT TEAM

"I am prepared to go anywhere — provided it be forward."

– David Livingston, 1875

OCTOBER 2012 – DAVIS, CALIFORNIA

Throughout the remainder of a busy 2012 MET season, I debriefed the Bodfish Creek mission internally numerous times. I grew fixated on finding ways to do the job more effectively and safely. The need for two significant changes became evident.

First, we needed specialized K9s like Phebe, dedicated to DTO suspect-apprehension roles. Since the Bodfish Creek operation, our team had been involved in four OIS incidents, and narrowly avoided another 20 or more since beginning targeted suspect-apprehension missions in 2005. Most of those gunfights, as illustrated during the Croy Road mission just a few weeks earlier, could have been avoided with K9 support.

Live-fire K9 drills during a MET tactical training session.

HIDDEN WAR

Second, we needed specialized wildlife-protection operators without distractions or red tape from above. D.N.'s directive to attend that meeting during the Bodfish Creek operation was the tipping point. His beliefs perfectly illustrated our Law Enforcement Division's (LED) traditional mindset concerning game warden involvement with DTO grow operations. Since our agency became involved in the DEA-sponsored statewide Committee Against Marijuana Planting (CAMP) program in 2005, this problem grew worse with each passing year. For a strategy against this environmental threat to be effective, the traditional LED mindset needed to change.

After years of fighting resistance to our efforts in DTO trespass marijuana enforcement, the time was finally right for change. With a new Northern Enforcement District assistant chief at the top, I reached out for a meeting. My partner for the progressive-operator concept was Capt. Nate, whom I had teamed up with for the first time on a DTO trespass cultivation operation in 2008. Nate and I worked great together, sharing the same vision, passion and relentless energy to tackle the most devastating environmental crimes from clandestine cartel cultivations.

Following the success of the Fay Creek operation, we knew we needed a specialized unit of highly trained game wardens free to work similar operations statewide, without district boundaries or traditional duties slowing them down. We presented a radical concept, but knowing the progressive-minded and persuasive nature of our new chief, we were confident he'd like the idea.

Given my background and experience in special operations team building, training and equipment, I covered the team-development and tactical-operations side of the proposal. This included team member selection, operational logistics, training, allied-agency integration and specialized equipment needs. With Nate's extensive experience as an incident commander on allied-agency DTO marijuana operations in the Central Enforcement District (CED), he had the command structure blueprint and statistics to justify our proposal.

Nate related pertinent figures from our involvement in each DTO trespass grow operation mission (number of marijuana plants removed, suspects caught, firearms and other weapons seized, length of water-diverting poly irrigation pipe removed, number and quantity of fertilizers found, banned and toxic chemicals found, number of dams removed, amount of trash on site, etc.). We pointed out that only a small percentage of grow operations involving our game wardens were being documented. These inaccurate, low figures reduced the amount of

This photo, taken during the pilot program's first tactical training session in 2013, marks a watershed moment. The author is pictured bottom row, second from the right.

DEA grant money our agency received each year to fund marijuana operations. Even worse, the figures underrepresented the number of trespass grows game wardens work, and the devastating environmental impacts associated.

Another issue we addressed at the meeting was the need for consistent statewide training and equipment for our officers when working marijuana ops. Although some of us integrated effectively with allied-agency spec ops teams, many of our officers lacked the specialized equipment needed to do the job safely. The days of five different state districts working marijuana operations in a hodgepodge of patrol equipment and personally purchased, gifted or borrowed tactical gear needed to end. Given the violent and dangerous nature of DTO growers and their complexes, the common practice of solo wardens scouting grow sites also needed to change.

The chief agreed. We were pleased when he directed us to test the specialized-team concept for a full summer. We needed to develop a pilot program for the 2013 season by building a team comprised of the most experienced and motivated operators. The gloves were off, and I could select operators without restrictions.

We knew this would rattle some supervisory cages. Team member selection would remove some of the best, most experienced patrol wardens from their home districts for the three-month pilot program. Regardless, we committed ourselves to making it happen. Not since our LED's covert undercover unit formed more than 30 years ago had a special operations team within the CDFW been built for a targeted environmental crime-fighting purpose.

For the next six months, we prepared for the upcoming team-selection process. The green light came in January of 2013. We needed tacticians with exceptional shooting, stalking, camouflage, defensive-tactics, arrest-and-control and outdoor fieldcraft skills. With my 20-year tenure and teaching experience, I had trained or worked with most of our state's 400 game wardens. I knew a lot of good shooters and arrest tacticians with great outdoor fieldcraft skills. I was looking for other critical character traits as well.

Team members needed to commit 100 percent and thrive on training. Compared to our statewide Peace Officer Standards and Training (POST) requirements, we were increasing the amount of training by 90 percent annually — an unprecedented amount for LED officers. And although we would certainly be questioned about training so much by the traditional-minded ranks, the violent and dangerous nature of our targeted criminals demanded it. Special operations teams all over the world knew the only thing separating them from mainline forces is training, and we needed this mindset from the beginning.

The fact that other anti-DTO teams throughout the country would take notice was another benefit. Plus, we would be a more capable, effective, and available resource when partnering with federal, state and local allied agencies on these missions.

JANUARY 2013 – SAN JOSE, CALIFORNIA

I started making calls late on a Friday afternoon. By early the following week, I garnered commitments from everyone we wanted on board.

From the Northern Enforcement District (NED) came Markos, Viking, Rumble and K9 Phebe, and Cardo and K9 Kilo — all solid operators who worked MET operations throughout northern California for years. These officers would be responsible for an area spanning from the Sacramento Valley north and east to the Oregon and Nevada borders. From our North

Coast District (NCD), we had Quinn, Jerry, Hendy and me covering all the coastal and inland counties, starting from the Monterey County coastline and extending north to the Oregon border.

From our Central Enforcement District, we were fortunate to have Shang and Frog covering from the Central Valley east and over the Sierra Nevada Range to the Nevada border. Shang was a skilled, quick-thinking operator who could build almost any improvised device needed for MET operations. Frog, a 20-year veteran of the SEAL teams, was new to our agency, but his decade-long tenure working narcotics operations as a Department of Justice (DOJ) agent was invaluable.

From the Southern Enforcement District (SED), starting in Ventura County and extending all the way south to the Mexican border, we had Cole and Mak — both young, skilled and motivated cadet academy mates of Quinn and Jerry.

Following team member selection, I dove into securing the specialized equipment we needed and began developing advanced MET training for our unit. We focused on tactical shooting, K9 operations, arrest-and-control and numerous other small-unit, mission-specific tactics tailored to any environment throughout the state.

We would also step up our physical conditioning, both on and off duty. With Frog at the helm of our curriculum, we got our asses kicked, SEAL team-style. With regimens including cross-country and hill runs, log carries, obstacle courses and relentless calisthenics, everyone improved their strength and physical endurance.

With all of us still assigned to our regular patrol districts, and with a minimal budget, some creative financing was necessary to get the team properly equipped. Several generous supporters and conservation friends provided new BDU combat uniforms, hats, boots and specialized patches. Meanwhile, Nate and I worked with the Sacramento HQ command staff to secure more ammunition and other equipment.

Given the amount of training required, we needed much more rifle and pistol ammo than normally allotted to district patrol wardens. Thankfully, the HQ training lieutenant located a stash of carbine and pistol ammo for us. He also fast-tracked the purchase of Safariland's best plate carrier, kit and specialized radio accessories. For the first time since any of us began working DTO cultivation operations, we were equipped with the right gear for maximum officer safety, mission survival and operational success.

The timing of our new equipment acquisition took place on the heels of a recent statewide rifle replacement and transition program. Since 2002, all LED officers carried either a military-issued M14 or M1A scout rifle for all assignments, including spec ops marijuana operations. Having co-developed the M14/M1A training program and carried a reliable and life-saving mil-spec M14 on duty for more than a decade, I was aware of the advantages and disadvantages of the platform.

Although it's a great rifle for reliability and stopping power, the M14 has some drawbacks, especially for special operations use in densely wooded terrain. I found navigating with it through thick underbrush difficult, given its length and weight. The lack of modularity and the difficulty of attaching optics, lights and other accessories to the platform presented tactical disadvantages — problems I experienced during our first gunfight in the Silicon Valley foothills in 2005.

Even when reducing the M14's barrel from 22 to 18 inches (the length of the M1A Scout's barrel), the rifle is still unwieldy. We even added VLTOR collapsible stocks and replaced the rifle's heat shield fore-ends with Picatinny rails to mount Aimpoint Micro H-1 red-dot sights. The M14 was still heavy and challenging to maneuver.

I was fortunate to be one of the Firearms Committee and Training leaders to choose a replacement. Like the M14, the systems needed to be chambered in 7.62 NATO, given our large-animal dispatching and barrier-penetration needs. After a 6,000-round torture test of the rifle samples submitted, Patriot Ordnance Factory's (POF) P308 was the only one to pass the rigorous requirements. It secured the contract.

Although not a light rifle, the modularity and compact size made the gun much better for our needs. We shaved almost a pound off our total battle kit weight — a significant weight reduction, given our operating environment. Ounces equal pounds and pounds equal pain while working where we do.

Our 14.5-inch-barreled, flash-hider-equipped P308s were colored in OD green with Flat Dark Earth furniture and accessories. With the addition of Aimpoint Micro red-dot sights, SureFire X300 Ultra LED weapon lights, TangoDown QD stubby vertical foregrips, Diamondhead backup iron-sight systems and VTAC padded two-point slings, the systems were equipped for any need. For agency personalization and pride, our game warden badge was laser engraved on the carbines' magazines.

In 2018, after five years of running the P308, we upgraded to POF's Revolution. As a custom-built featherweight 7.62 NATO carbine the size of a 5.56 platform, this carbine shaved another 2 pounds off of our total kit weight. A godsend for MET operators, the Revolution was a pleasure to shoot and carry on long stalks in the bush.

APRIL 2013 – SANTA CLARA COUNTY SHERIFF'S RANGE

With all the necessary equipment in hand, we started training. In addition to our own internal team's practice, we conducted an allied-agency MET-operations training with Spag's team at the Santa Clara County MET in April 2013. Because successful suspect-apprehension and trespass grow site tactics developed hand-in-hand with the Santa Clara County MET, the opportunity

Markos works overwatch during the Bake Oven-Lunch Meadow DTO grow complex operation.

to work together with other like-minded operators was exciting. We covered advanced-trauma medicine, small-unit tactical shooting and movement, live-fire grow assaults, officer and hostage rescue and K9 apprehension drills, in addition to land navigation, stalking, fieldcraft and camouflage.

After our MET's kickoff training evolution, Nate busied himself finding a high-profile, focused operation for us to work. Our special operations military counter-drug task force allies from the California Air National Guard's (CANG) Team Hawk reached out to partner up with us for the upcoming season. Between its Mather and Moffett air bases, the 129th Air Rescue Squadron had Black Hawk and Pave Hawk helicopters, flight crews, an entire ground unit of overseas combat veterans and logistical support dedicated to working anti-DTO trespass cultivation operations every day of August 2013. They needed the right agency partner for the mission, and we were happy to oblige.

Given the focus of this mission in environmentally sensitive watersheds and lands, we dubbed the detail Operation PRISTINE (Protecting Resources Involving Specialized Teams in Narcotics Enforcement) — a fitting title to illustrate our unique environmental protection approach.

Along with Team Hawk, we also utilized reclamation volunteers from our own agency's Natural Resource Volunteer Program (NRVP). These dedicated civilians offered their time to the long, arduous process of DTO grow site reclamation and cleanup. Their assistance on the month-long mission would be invaluable.

We started operations without patrol district distractions following the July 4th holiday. Our MET operators worked allied-agency DTO operations in their assigned areas of responsibility that first week, documenting environmental crimes and overseeing the reclamation process on each mission, which most allied-agency teams were not familiar with. Although we caught more bad guys when working with these teams, the real rewards were the data we collected and the grow waste, irrigation line, water diversions, pesticides, fertilizers and other grow site poisons we removed.

Although reluctant at first, we soon had most sheriff's department and narcotics task force teams reclamating grow sites with us all over the state. We sold the idea as a simple trade: we'll help you catch bad guys with our tactics and K9s and eradicate plants, if you help us restore the environmental damage left behind. Doing so would not only clean up the environment, but also deter another DTO crew from setting up in that same area.

Our reclamation-deterrence theory was solid. We witnessed this trend firsthand, and we had intelligence to back it up. An apprehended DTO grow boss responsible for numerous northern California trespass grow sites confirmed what we had suspected for years. With incentives for his cooperation, he provided us with valuable intelligence into the mindset of DTO grow operators throughout the country.

When asked if reclamation made a difference in his operations, he confirmed it did. The decision to reestablish a grow operation was a simple cost/benefit analysis calculation to determine whether the risk outweighed the potential reward. If a complex were only eradicated, his crews would return to that area and use the existing infrastructure (water diversions, irrigation systems, gardening tools, camp and kitchen supplies, etc.) to reestablish the operation.

If the site was reclamated, however, the incentives to grow there again disappeared. With the site already on law enforcement's radar, and the need to put tens of thousands of dollars into a new water supply and other infrastructure, the risk wasn't worth it. This boss's perspective affirmed not only the environmental resource-protection value of conducting trespass grow reclamations, but the deterrence value of doing so as well. This helped our MET show the numerous allied-agency teams the importance of reclamation operations.

Other intel the grow boss provided was not so positive. For years, we'd been curious why so many DTO operatives that our team apprehended were illegally in the United States from Mexico. Most came from the central-highlands area of Michoacán. Why was it so easy for these criminals to get across the border and run clandestine grow operations?

The boss grinned at these questions and told us the border was not even recognized by the DTOs as a dividing line between countries. They consider California part of Mexico, referring to it as "Mexico Norte" (Mexico North). They see the border as a minor roadblock. DTO cartel groups run operations throughout California and the rest of the United States as if the border doesn't even exist. They send up skilled and vetted veteran growers from Mexico who proved their effectiveness. For a relatively small fee of $4,000 to $7,000, cartel bosses get their best growers, gunmen and transporters across the border easily. Even if operatives are detained and deported, they can be smuggled across the border again within days.

Equally alarming was how growers smuggle containers of EPA-banned, Carbofuran-based poisons into the United States when they cross. Illegal and unavailable in the States, DTO groups simply buy the product in Tijuana and run it into the United States with their growers. Fast, effective and trouble-free, the cartels move as many personnel and grow poisons into the country as they need. Worse, these groups also cook meth, work in the heroin and fentanyl markets, run human-trafficking operations and smuggle stolen guns and ammunition back to Mexico to fuel fights between cartel factions. Given their easy, covert access into the United States, DTO cartels linked up to extreme terrorist groups committed to wreaking havoc on American soil.

Although frustrating, this intel proved valuable. It validated our suspicions and illuminated the larger threat these organized crime groups pose throughout the country.

JULY 2013 – STATEWIDE THROUGHOUT CALIFORNIA

The July kickoff ran nonstop, with our operators involved in missions statewide each day of the week. The team generated record numbers in all

A Marijuana Enforcement Team (MET) agent maintains overnight suspect security and dries rain-soaked gear during the Bake Oven-Lunch Meadow operation.

categories: plants eradicated, suspects caught, firearms seized, amount of grow site trash removed, number of water diversions restored, amount of irrigation pipe and chemicals removed, etc. Those figures told an alarming story.

We discovered the use of EPA-banned poisons like Carbofuran, Furdan, Furadan, Metafos and their derivatives in more than 75 percent of our missions. Before the season, we reasoned these figures would be high, but until our analyst totaled up the yields from each mission, we couldn't be sure. Calculating hard figures throughout the pilot program was essential, because we had to show chiefs throughout the state the depth of the problem.

Environmental research conducted in the private sector into DTO grow complexes also helped prosecute trespass grow cases throughout the country. Although we documented the widespread poisoning of wildlife and waterways for years, we hadn't quantified these damages until recently.

Right before we launched our pilot program, Integral Ecology Research Center (IERC) scientists began working with our agency's MET and the U.S. Forest Service in grow complexes throughout California. IERC's research was the first to scientifically document the toxic effects of these poisons on grow complex wildlife and waterways. Its research showed how the Pacific fisher was almost wiped out from widespread use of these substances, and the finding received national attention from policymakers. IERC's work generated funding for more research, reclamation operations and the development of safety protocols for those of us working within these toxic sites.

AUGUST 2013 - SEQUOIA NATIONAL FOREST - TULARE COUNTY, CALIFORNIA

Our MET just started Operation PRISTINE with the CANG when we received a request for support from the Tulare County Sheriff's Office and the U.S. Forest Service (USFS). My long-time USFS special agent colleague and friend, B.A., identified two DTO trespass grow sites within the most remote area of the Sequoia National Forest. The two grow targets were in a wilderness area home to sensitive mammal species and the California golden trout, which is listed as a California "species of concern."

That these two sites (Bake Oven and Lunch Meadow) were just below 10,000 feet in elevation presented some unusual challenges. An 8-mile cross-country hike above timberline presented the shortest route. This required a long insertion on foot, with an overnight listening post/observation post set up before raiding the two sites the following day. The grows were a few miles apart. They required two separate entry teams to set up on the edge of each the following morning before hitting targets simultaneously at first light. Our radio communications would be sketchy between our two teams that far apart.

The fact that we would be out overnight, close to our targets, with no air support from the CANG, was another challenge. With the air so thin and temperatures so high at our altitude, the Black Hawk would drink almost an entire tank of fuel just to fly between the 7,000-foot-elevation landing zone, to the grow site locations and back. Given the fuel consumption issue, the flight crew decided to fly into the target area the following morning from a more helicopter-friendly airbase in the Central Valley flatlands. Bottom line, we were without air support or other backup until the next morning. We were on our own if things got western before then.

Following our midday ops briefing in a well-hidden campground high up in the Sequoia National Forest, both entry teams traveled to the drop point — a well-camouflaged trailhead B.A. had discovered several weeks earlier. As case agent, and the person most familiar with the terrain, B.A. was our point man leading both entry teams. Right behind him was Markos, followed by Rumble and K9 Phebe. I covered and followed our K9 team closely, with Shang and Frog providing rifle support behind me. A few Tulare County deputies followed behind Frog, rounding out our Bake Oven contingent.

In the stack behind our Bake Oven team were Cole, Quinn, Jerry and several Tulare County deputies, all following Sergeant Jim, the Lunch Meadow team leader. Our teams would stay together until it was time to separate toward our LP/OP positions for both grow sites, 6 miles into the hike. Given the open granite and juniper/pine-covered terrain, we stretched out into a long ranger file and hiked toward the targeted sites. At the 6-mile separation point, B.A., Sergeant Jim and I stopped to review the plan one more time. We checked our communications again before our teams separated.

Less than two miles from the Bake Oven target, the wind picked up. Dark thunder clouds rolled in and the summer temperature dropped rapidly. Within 30 minutes, heavy rain and quarter-sized hail pounded our position at a wide-open, exposed ridgeline. The close lightning strikes and thunder rumbles that followed were both exciting and unnerving. We hovered at the base of the few trees we could find for cover. Given the weather conditions, we were confident the likelihood of encountering suspects on the trail ahead was low.

The California Air National Guard's 129th Air Rescue Squadron Black Hawk helicopter extracts a cartel suspect during the Bake Oven-Lunch Meadow operation.

Or so we thought.

With the rain settling down, we moved off the exposed ridgeline and entered a wet, sandy wash. Just then, B.A. and Rumble spotted someone ahead. Soaked head to toe and headed straight for us were two armed DTO growers, dressed in U.S. government-issue camouflage BDUs. As surprised to see us as we were them, the men turned and ran before any of us could announce and identify ourselves.

K9 Phebe already had a lock on the men. Rumble unleashed the Fur Missile, giving her the command to apprehend. Her blazing speed closed the gap on the runners in a blink. She tackled and apprehended one man, sending her target tumbling onto the sandy wash below. The second man made it around a bend out of sight — too far ahead and past uncleared terrain — preventing us from pursuing him.

Markos and Rumble searched and assessed the suspect for injuries. Falling in behind our K9 runners, the rest of us positioned into a 360 formation and took a knee before I called for a team SITREP.

During Rumble's quick interview of the suspect, the grower told us he and his partner were the only two working the Bake Oven grow site. Despite the storm, they had left the grow to hike to the Lunch Meadow complex to borrow food from their colleagues. A bear had ransacked their camp and kitchen, decimating their supply.

We considered our options and decided to set up an overnight camp in the wash and push on early the next morning as planned. We didn't need to take the risk with no air support and the last light of day fading quickly. Our element of surprise was gone, and an ambush could be waiting at the Bake Oven site.

Thankfully, the rain ended as we set up camp. Using an old-growth juniper tree and pinion pines to shelter us from the wind and secure our suspect, we built a fire to dry everyone's soaked clothing and gear as darkness fell. Rumble and B.A. recorded the suspect's interview on a camcorder. Frog, Shang and Markos held our 360-degree perimeter around camp.

We built the MET to handle these types of unpredictable and challenging situations, and we were thriving on the mission. We had chosen the term "fill and flow" as our team motto at the inception of the pilot program, and here we were, alone and without support, filling and flowing into any contingency in one of the most pristine and remote regions of the state. Proud and satisfied, my grin yielded to the vast blanket of stars above as I wondered what tomorrow's raid would yield.

Our team rolled out at 0430 hours the following morning. B.A., Rumble, Frog, Shang and the task force deputies started their hike to the Bake Oven grow site well before first light. Markos and I stayed back in camp, maintaining security of our suspect and facilitating his air extraction later that morning. The grower grew restless and had the familiar caged-animal look of a prisoner ready to make a break for it. We watched him carefully until our air support arrived.

Just after first light, the entry team reached the Bake Oven target and found the grow abandoned, with the kitchen and camp torn apart by a bear, just as the grower had stated. We found several calibers of handgun and rifle ammunition throughout the complex, but none of the associated firearms were found. It appeared our prisoner's companion was long gone.

The grow contained more than 7,000 mature marijuana plants, and it completely dewatered the pristine creek that paralleled the complex. Our team also found several empty and partially used containers of the EPA-banned poison Carbofuran throughout the site, indicating the plants, soil and irrigation water was tainted.

At approximately 0930 hours, Markos and I heard the welcome thump of rotor blades from the CANG's Black Hawk. I made radio contact with the pilot to vector him in. Markos retrieved the bright orange air panel from my pack and placed it on the ground to mark our position. The pilot told us that given the thin air and rising temperature, his crew only had enough fuel to hoist our suspect into the chopper with a longline cable and get him back to the landing zone before they needed to fly off-station and refuel. He wasn't sure if he could return to hoist us out of the grow after refueling.

Realizing we'd likely be backtracking 8 miles on foot back to yesterday's drop point, I checked our supplies while Markos maintained security of the suspect. With both of us low on water and the day heating up quickly, we prepared to hike out on foot.

The Black Hawk moved into a deafening hover above us, flattening the surrounding vegetation and kicking up a blinding dust storm from the 100-mph rotor wash winds. The crew knew we were getting pounded on the ground and dropped a rescue screamer suit (a nylon body-wrapping blanket used to hoist untrained personnel safely into the helicopter) before pulling away as quickly as possible. I maintained my grip on the suspect, keeping him locked in a bent-wrist control hold around his handcuffs. Markos ran down the wash to retrieve the screamer suit. If the bad guy wanted to run, he would try it now.

Within minutes, we had the suspect strapped into the suit and taking the most exciting ride of his life to jail. The crew chief hoisted him up toward the big hovering Black Hawk airship. One of the wardens waited inside to take him into custody. Seconds after the grower was inside the helicopter, and with every second of flight time sucking down more of the big ship's fuel reserves, the pilot broke his hover and directed the ship southeast toward the landing zone.

In silence for the first time in days, Markos and I stood in the wash and paused for a minute, taking in the pristine, granite-based forest around us. Clean and crisp from the recent rainstorm, the area's environmental sensitivity was visible everywhere. Although we should have seen several mule deer and other mammals that reside in the area, we hadn't seen a single animal all morning — and we knew why. Just before we started our hike, the pilot called us on the radio. After dropping the suspect and our custody officer back at the landing zone, he had just enough fuel to hoist and fly us out. God bless our military pilots and their commitment to leaving no team member behind! The fuel burn was so tight that we would be flying with his crew all the way to Inyokern to refuel before returning to the landing zone and our patrol vehicles — a long flight we were happy to take.

In the Bake Oven grow, B.A. accompanied Rumble and K9 Phebe to document and map out the complex for B.A.'s criminal case against the suspect. In the process, they also cleared the site of booby traps, weapons and any other officer safety threats. Frog, Shang and the task force officers eradicated and reclamated most of the site, rectifying the water diversion before leaving. With the small stream's flow restored, the team prepared for exfiltration by helicopter. By the end of the afternoon, we were clear and safe from the operation, and conveying home over the southeastern Sierras. We felt exhausted, but we were pleased with the results of such a challenging and exciting detail.

As of this writing almost five years later, the Bake Oven-Lunch Meadow operation remains one of our most challenging, and one of the most significant. Because the mission occurred so early in the pilot program and showed many key allied agencies our capabilities, the outcome paved the way for our acceptance and success in DTO trespass grow operations all over the state. I'll never forget the excitement and positive attitudes shared by our operators when executing Operation PRISTINE.

We worked almost every day since the July startup, completing statewide operations, scout missions, mission planning, tactical training and numerous outreach presentations. We teamed up with not only our CANG military partners, but more than 100 county, state and federal allied agencies.

We generated some impressive numbers during the three-month test period. By the end of the pilot program, our MET completed 182 arrest, eradication and reclamation missions. We eradicated 507,160 poisoned, black-market marijuana plants and destroyed 7,429 pounds of tainted marijuana in the process. During those operations, we captured 235 DTO operatives (most of them armed with a gun, knife or both) and seized 77 firearms from grow complexes. During environmental reclamation, we removed 38.5 tons of grow waste and trash, 65 miles of black poly irrigation pipe, 9.4 tons of water-poisoning fertilizers and 134 containers of EPA-banned poisons. When rectifying water diversions found on site, we removed 129 dams responsible for stealing millions of gallons of water during a major drought period.

With these figures representing only a three-month period and knowing we had worked only a fraction of the DTO grow sites in the state, the magnitude of the problem came into clear view. After so many missions, with so many public safety threats and vast environmental decimation, we were all eager to keep rolling and take the team to the next level as a sanctioned, dedicated unit.

Fortunately, that's exactly what happened. The MET would be a permanent unit. While we were ready to pitch the idea following the pilot program's conclusion, neither Nate nor I expected it to happen so fast. Our chief wanted position testing developed and conducted before the end of the year. By Jan. 1, 2014, the MET should be operational under the Sacramento headquarters' special operations umbrella. We would be free from district boundaries and patrol division red tape, allowing quick decisions and logistical support for a team that needed to move and operate quickly to be effective. Nate and I dove in immediately.

NOVEMBER 2013 - CDFW HEADQUARTERS - SACRAMENTO, CALIFORNIA

Regardless of our involvement in building and running the MET through the pilot program, Nate and I still had to compete against statewide LED applicants interested in the MET lieutenant and captain positions. The embarrassment of not being selected for the position after everything we had done to make the team a reality would be unbearable. Fortunately, we both accepted offers to run the team.

DECEMBER 2013 - SANTA CLARA COUNTY SHERIFF'S RANGE

Two weeks before Christmas, we conducted panel interviews and grow site scenario testing for MET operator positions at the Santa Clara County sheriff's range. With Spag, Snake, Rails, Hunter and Miya assisting in scenario evaluations, we tested 20 applicants for 12 positions over a two-day period. Except for one officer, everyone from the pilot program tested for a full-time position, and selections were made the following week. By the holiday break, the first dedicated conservation officer DTO environmental crime-fighting team in our nation's history was official.

While our forte was DTO trespass operations in remote outdoor environments, everyone came certified and experienced in SWAT-related tactical operations. As a result, the MET morphed into a rapid-response tactical unit able to deploy in any environment for any high-risk mission our agency demands.

MET's craft and proficiency included high-risk indoor entry operations; vehicle interdiction and assault missions; urban, rural and high-altitude rappelling and ascending; horse and mule operations; OHV specialized-vehicle tactics; active-shooter response, man-tracking and fugitive recovery; advanced helicopter operations (aerial gunning, spy line, hoist and short-haul operations); night-vision goggle (NVG) ops; covert-entry tactics; advanced arrest-control and ground-fighting techniques; and offshore marine tactical missions, including large- and small-vessel interdiction and on-water shooting tactics.

Like other domestic law enforcement tactical teams, the MET stood ready to integrate with any other agency on homeland security issues. We trained for this contingency constantly. As I will discuss in a following chapter, we developed a sniper/observer team within the MET, capable of handling any urban or rural precision rifle and long-range surveillance needs during operations.

CHAPTER 05

MISSION *EL DIABLO*: DEADLY POISONS AND DROUGHT IMPACTS ON THE SAN JOAQUIN RIVER

"We go into the night as brave men go.
Our faces often streaked with woe.

As we've danced with death a
dozen times or so..."

— Rhyme of the Restless Ones, by Robert Service

JULY 2015 – SAN JOAQUIN RIVER – CROWS LANDING, CALIFORNIA

Positioned on a large peninsula, surrounded by the mighty San Joaquin River, the forest sanctuary so many wild animals once called home was hardly recognizable. A labyrinth of manmade trails crisscrossed all directions. Thousands of bright-green marijuana plants in organized rows replaced the brush- and tree-choked grassy meadows. Hoses on the ground emitted water to the base of each plant, and an odd chemical smell permeated the air. Any thirsty animals, such as the mule deer common to this area, that licked up cold relief from the plant's base could seize up and die from the nerve toxin-tainted water.

Many did.

Five months later ...

Cruising in the northbound fast lane of Highway 99, Shang was en route to assess another DTO grow site for an end-of-the-year reclamation operation. Along with the rest of our team, he was at the tail end of a busy 2015 MET season. He tried to wind down for the holidays, but it wasn't easy. Even in late December, calls about grow sites still came in.

We worked large-scale marijuana grow operations within the remote waterways of the Sacramento Delta that year — a first for us. With California's historic drought peaking in its third year, and with traditional DTO waterways bone dry because of it, grower teams all over the state shifted operations to areas with more water. Embedded throughout the thick, jungle-like riparian waterways of the Delta, cartel crews had the water and concealment they needed to push through the drought, making our enforcement efforts even more challenging.

Shang approached the turnoff to his target area when his cell phone rang. Seeing that it was Jeffe, an allied-agency colleague from the Stanislaus Drug Enforcement Agency (SDEA) and helicopter operations expert, he answered immediately. Jeffe's team received a tip from a neighboring county about a large harvested grow site adjacent to the San Joaquin River, just inside the Stanislaus County line near Crows Landing. It had been spotted from the air and looked big.

The news made Shang concerned. The San Joaquin River is one of the last anadromous fisheries left in our state, home to migrating steelhead. It also served as a drinking water and irrigation source for legitimate agriculture in the region. The potential negative effects on wildlife, crops and people downstream were alarming.

Shang's curiosity couldn't wait. He fired up his laptop at home and drafted a scout plan to assess the grow. To scout the site safely, he reached out to Tony, one of our MET alternate teammates in the area. Within 12 hours of discussing the scout plan, Shang and Tony stood only 50 yards from the suspected grow coordinates. Kneeling in the levy's tall grass, with their carbines at the low ready, they scanned for threats. A 20-foot-wide, flooded slough separated them from the riparian belt above the levee. They had no choice but to cross it. Unsure of the murky water's depth, and knowing that the slough mud was like quicksand, they couldn't risk trying to cross it directly on foot.

K9 Phebe, aka the "Fur Missile," in ambush position along a large plot of poisoned marijuana in the Crows Landing DTO grow complex.

While Tony covered with his carbine, Shang broke concealment and moved along the water's edge, looking for a way to safely cross the slough. Fifty yards downstream, he lucked out and spotted a large willow tree. With its large trunk rooted on the peninsula side of the channel, one of the old willow's largest branches spanned across the entire slough, positioned for an improvised bridge. Hopefully it could take the weight of two operators decked out in heavy armor and weapon kits without snapping and sending Shang and Tony into the murky current.

Shang attempted the crossing first, with Tony covering their backtrail on the levee side of the slough. Like walking a tightrope, using his carbine as a balancing pole, Shang moved across the waterway, the powerful flow just inches from his boot soles. After a few slips and recoveries, he made it

Training is essential to success. Here's an example of steep mountain helicopter toe-in infill and exfil training.

HIDDEN WAR

to the peninsula, relieved and unscathed before covering Tony's crossing next. With both operators safely on the bank, they took a knee, scanned and listened for human movement ahead. After five minutes of only the Delta's abundant wildlife sounds, Shang stepped toward the target coordinates, with Tony following a few yards behind.

Although some grow site tips yield inaccurate locations, these coordinates were spot on. Shang and Tony penetrated the dense forest that separated the grow complex from the slough and stopped in shock. As far as they could see, thousands of holes containing cut and harvested marijuana plants riddled the fertile ground. Black poly pipe irrigation line ran up and down the edges of the entire plot. The plot measured almost 100 yards long and at least 50 yards wide. Both men noticed numerous well-worn human trails leading in all directions to other parts of the forested peninsula. Experience told them that these trails led to the site's other marijuana plots, camps and kitchens associated with this Goliath complex. Saw marks darkened on tree limbs also indicated this complex had been active for several years.

Judging by the size of the plot alone, and knowing each plant required 10 to 12 gallons of water per day for 150 days until harvest to thrive, the amount of water this complex diverted from the San Joaquin River was staggering. Worse yet, Shang and Tony saw numerous empty containers of the EPA-banned poison, Carbofuran, stashed in the bases of small trees throughout the plot. The complex turned toxic when *el Diablo* poison was used in large quantities for the growing season. The devastation to the fish and wildlife in the area could only be immense. The scout team knew the growers would be back the following season to milk this cash cow for all the millions of black-market dollars it was worth.

Shang looked at Tony in disgust. With no need to push farther into the grow site and risk leaving tracks or other sign, they covered their tracks on their way out. Away from the grow complex, Shang called me with a SITREP. I could hear both the excitement and disgust in his voice as he walked me through their find. My heart raced with rage and excitement. Shang and I agreed this site needed to be a top priority for our team next season. This site not only marked one of the biggest we've encountered, but also the most polluted. The environmental criminals running it wreaked unprecedented havoc on the pristine San Joaquin watershed for many years.

It was time to shut the site down for good.

Spy line infill and exfil training with the Stanislaus County airship. Helicopters are the backbone of operations in remote areas and are a major advantage.

LATE APRIL 2016

Early next season, we started work on the Crows Landing case, conducting flyovers with Jeffe and his SDEA aircrew. They spotted thousands of plants spread out all over the peninsula, confirming the site was active again for the 2016 season. The complex proved much larger than we anticipated. Taking it down couldn't wait. Shang, Tony, Jeffe and I developed an ops plan and gathered personnel and resources.

We needed a lot of personnel and air and land vehicle assets. We were thankful to have support from Jeffe and his SDEA colleagues, as well as the Stanislaus County SWAT team, narcotics officers and our military allies with the CANG. Although our takedown plan contained a lot of moving parts, we felt confident we could pull it off by dividing into teams to handle each task. As case agent, Shang ran the investigation and performed the heavy lifting on behalf of our MET — his biggest challenge yet.

> Thousands of bright-green marijuana plants in organized rows replaced the brush- and tree-choked grassy meadows. Hoses on the ground emitted water to the base of each plant, and an odd chemical smell permeated the air. Any thirsty animals, such as the mule deer common to this area, that licked up cold relief from the plant's base could seize up and die from the nerve toxin-tainted water.

Our team became the entry and apprehension group responsible for clearing the entire complex. No other team was permitted into the grow site until we secured the entire area. This lessened the chance or Mr. Murphy screwing up our operation and avoided blue-on-blue casualties.

Stanislaus County SWAT would function as our perimeter team, surrounding the complex to catch any runners. We considered runners a given.

A rarity on most of our operations, we were lucky to have separate eradication and reclamation teams on the mission. Comprised of Jeffe's SDEA colleagues, fellow narcotics team members and the CANG, this inter-agency group would stand by and stay clear of the complex until our MET and Stanislaus County SWAT locked it down and cleared it of any suspects or other threats.

We slated Jeffe and the aircrews from the Stanislaus County Sheriff's Office to provide overwatch during the takedown. They would also assist us with plant and grow site waste removal during the eradication and reclamation phases of the operation. Given the size of the complex, these would be the most challenging and arduous tasks of the day.

Another challenge involved working with FOX News for an investigative feature story. FOX reached out to me the previous year to do a story on the DTOs' use of Carbofuran-based EPA-banned poisons, as well as the drought impacts and other environmental crimes associated with illegal marijuana grow operations. Given the size of the site and the confirmed presence of vast amounts of poisonous chemicals, the operation had all of the concerns associated with DTO grow operations, making it ideal to share with the FOX media crew.

Fortunately, the geography around the target favored the mission. With the entire complex on a peninsula and surrounded on three sides by the San Joaquin River and deep sloughs, suspect apprehension potential seemed high.

EARLY MAY 2016

Our entry team huddled shoulder-to-shoulder in a large circle a few miles from the target site. Concealed at the end of a remote dirt road at 4 a.m., and with copies of our operations plan illuminated by headlamps, everyone listened while Shang and I broke down the plan for the day. Shang stressed its enormity and the widespread presence of Carbofuran-based poisons. I addressed the officer safety dangers we might encounter. We required night vision goggles (NVGs) to navigate the flooded levy to the edge of the grow site and to anticipate armed growers, tripwires, punji pits, pit traps, noise-makers and quicksand-like mud. The entry phase would be one of the most challenging parts of the operation.

A CDFW MET operator moves into an overwatch position during training. Game wardens with special training and equipment are needed to deal with the cartels' fully funded grower teams. Imagine what can happen when unsuspecting families inadvertently hike into an illegal grow site on public land and run into a gang of heavily armed cartel operatives.

Ten minutes after the briefing, we jumped into two patrol trucks and drove two miles to the starting point of our hike. We rolled in blacked out using infrared lighting systems and NVGs. Invisible to the human eye, infrared lighting looks like bright headlights for normal night driving when viewed through NVGs. The technology allowed us to travel in complete darkness as if it were daytime and increased our concealment, officer safety and element of surprise.

We parked off the levee road near the drop point and exited our trucks before stacking up into our point apprehension and secondary Quick Reaction Force (QRF) formations. Shang and Tony went up front on point with their carbines. Rumble, K9 Phebe, Markos and I followed. Frog covered our six o'clock. Behind him, Mak positioned as point man for our QRF. Behind Mak on the QRF were Quinn, Tango and Cole, with Jerry covering the QRF's tail. A mile away, Stanislaus County SWAT moved in with its

Cartel grower spraying a deadly Carbofuran poison mix on mature marijuana plants.

NVGs to form our perimeter net.

Shang noticed how the drop point looked completely different in the middle of the night. Knowing how dangerous the creek crossing had been during his scout six months prior in daylight, he looked for a better crossing point. Frustrated after five minutes of searching the surrounding levy bank, he returned and told me the crossing point was gone and the water was much deeper now. Still, we had no choice but to cross it.

With his carbine held above chest level, Shang stepped off the levy and sunk to his chest in the murky water. Rocking back and forth to stay upright in the slough's current, and fighting to maintain his balance, our point man found stable footing in the slough's deep mud. I watched this all through the surreal green glow of my NVGs, and I noted how my limited depth perception added another challenge when it was my turn to cross. I breathed a sigh of relief when Shang finally made it across. One by one, the rest of us crossed carefully. Rumble cradled Phebe across his chest during his passage. Our point and QRF teams were soaking wet, but good to go.

Not far over the levy's bank waited one of the grow complex's main trails. Shang located it quickly. He navigated us through the thick line of vegetation hiding the trail. Now just a few minutes from sunrise, we stopped and held the team just inside the brush line. Everyone took a knee in the surrounding vegetation for concealment. We peeled our packs and secured our NVGs within them, transitioning to gear for an early morning, low-light hunt. Because we were working with FOX News, I also carried my small HD camcorder to capture footage of the grow site. Given the presence of banned poisons, we couldn't risk bringing media personnel into the site, even after it had been cleared and secured. It was up to us to get the interior footage needed to tell the worst part of the environmental destruction story.

A lot of our gear submerged during the slough crossing, so we conducted a final gear check. We moved out a few minutes later.

Well-worn trails peeled off on both sides of the path as we penetrated deeper into the heart of the grow complex. Clearly, the site had been in use for many years and was one of the largest any of us had ever seen. Within minutes, we moved through a large plot of marijuana plants. Dead cottontail rabbits and mourning doves at the base of several plants marked sure signs of Carbofuran use. Although we expected this, the high number of dead animals sickened us.

We continued to glide down the trail, witnessing more signs of environmental devastation. With my camcorder rolling point-of-view style, I captured the large black irrigation line diverting water from one of the many sloughs of the San Joaquin River into the heart of the grow. Seconds later, we passed a large, gas-powered water pump with a 3-inch hose line attached. Next to the pump sat a large, grower-built check dam containing a Molotov cocktail of discolored poisons in the stagnant water. Viewing through the camera, I fixated on the grotesque, rainbow-colored sheen of gasoline- and poison-tainted water. Suddenly, our pace picked up.

All hell broke loose when Shang and Rumble yelled, "Police! Put your hands up and don't move!"

Just past the poisoned waterhole, in the darkness of the tree canopy, Shang breached the entrance to a well-camouflaged, tarp-covered grower camp and kitchen, with everyone home. Waking up in their cots, all four growers were shocked when our team entered their lair.

Events turned western instantly.

Three of the four startled growers jumped out of their bunks in a flash, running barefoot in their underwear before crashing through the brush wall of their kitchen to escape. They were fast — really fast — with a clearly rehearsed escape plan, but we were ready for them. With pistols and numerous knives already identified in their camp upon our entry, Rumble released the Fur Missile. Giving her the command to apprehend, Phebe tackled the third grower after a 30-yard chase.

Rumble didn't hesitate and continued to sprint after the first two growers, yelling, "Send my dog! Send my dog!"

Tony released Phebe and yelled, "Good girl, good girl! Go, go, go!"

Rumble never looked back as he chased the two growers through their marijuana plots and into the head-high riparian grasslands. He hoped to push them toward the peninsula's boundary and right into the hands of our Stanislaus County SWAT perimeter operators and their K9.

Shang ran ahead of Rumble as fast as he could to catch the second fleeing suspect. Closing the gap and drawing his TASER with his support hand while maintaining control of his carbine with his strong hand, Shang got a shot at the grower 10 yards ahead. He pressed the TASER's trigger and launched two long-distance electronic probes toward the suspect, but to no effect. Dense levy grasses deflected both probes, and the grower sprinted farther into the thick grassland and disappeared. Stopping to switch cartridges on his TASER, Shang was hit in the thigh and surprised by the Fur Missile. Phebe shot past him in a blur, locked on target and still in pursuit of the grower. A second later, Rumble caught up to Shang and the two operators sprinted in tandem after Phebe.

As our QRF moved up in support, Markos, Frog, Mak, Quinn, Tango, Cole and Jerry held the camp and secured the growers' numerous weapons. I sprinted ahead. With plenty of operators in camp to secure the two suspects,

Shang checks the depth of a hand-dug well used for marijuana irrigation during the peak of California's drought. Illegal grows divert millions of gallons of scarce water.

we needed to provide Rumble and Shang with help should they encounter more threats.

I caught up to Rumble, Shang and Phebe at the base of the next levy a few seconds later and smiled as I caught my breath. Handcuffed on the ground in front of the Fur Missile was the second runner. In typical Phebe fashion, she locked her eyes on the grower, as if daring him to move. This apprehension was not hers alone; our Stanislaus County SWAT K9 handler and his K9, Smoke, stood concealed on top of the levy above. The fleeing grower nearly ran into them as he tried to skedaddle. The man surrendered before being

A helicopter removes some of the miles of water-diversion line from the Crows Landing DTO grow complex.

tackled by the dog — a safe ending for everyone involved.

Our celebration didn't last long. We needed to get back to the rest of our team and continue clearing the grow complex. While escorting the grower back to the camp, Rumble, Shang and I assessed the status of the first runner. None of us saw him after his initial sprint out of the camp, and we agreed he was too far away to track. Hopefully, the perimeter team would scoop him up as he tried to slip by, as we had a lot of un-cleared terrain ahead of us to secure.

Back at the camp, we kept the three growers separated and secured. We interviewed them within a few minutes. Tango and Cole treated them for numerous scrapes and bruises they received during their escape attempt.

With Tango and Jerry staying in camp to guard the suspects, we stacked back up into formation and headed out to clear the rest of the complex. For the next hour, we traveled nearly a quarter-mile through massive plots containing budded, Carbofuran-tainted plants. We documented numerous poisoned animal carcasses, including deer, cottontail rabbits, blue jays, mourning doves and other non-game birds.

While the rest of the team held formation on a trail, Frog and I followed a diversion path leading down to the San Joaquin River. Hidden along the bank and submerged in the river was the other end of the 3-inch waterline we found attached to the water pump near the first camp. Attached to the end of the line was a large filter, placed on the line to keep the pump from plugging up while diverting millions of gallons of the San Joaquin's water into the complex's multiple grow sites. We found three more massive water pump diversions within the complex.

After another hour of clearing the numerous trails throughout the complex, we found another well-worn trail leading to a thick, wooded depression on the opposite end of the peninsula. I pulled my pocket binoculars from my plate carrier. I rose up through the tall grass while Shang covered me with his carbine.

Peering through multiple layers of vegetation and tree limbs, I made out a camouflaged tarp covering another camp. After monitoring the camp for a few minutes and seeing no movement, I made the call to assault the camp from three sides and contain anyone still inside. If we were lucky, the growers would be out in another grow past the camp, still oblivious to our presence. If we were really lucky, they hadn't heard us and were still in camp, getting a late start to their day.

With rifle support on Rumble and Phebe, our K9 team moved up the trail toward the camp's center as carbine-supported light runners flanked both sides of the Fur Missile. We closed in on the camp in a skirmish line.

We got lucky. Four growers still slept in their cots. Using existing concealment within the camp, we continued to close the gap until one of the growers saw the Fur Missile stalking toward him. The shock of seeing a full team of silent, camouflaged and heavily armed spec ops warriors surrounding them deflated the growers' will to fight. They gave up instantly. Their surrender was surreal given the chaos with their associates in the other camp just a few hours earlier.

Judging by the size of the plot alone, and knowing each plant required 10 to 12 gallons of water per day for 150 days until harvest to thrive, the amount of water this complex diverted from the San Joaquin River was staggering. Worse yet, Shang and Tony saw numerous empty containers of the EPA-banned poison, Carbofuran, stashed in the bases of small trees throughout the plot ... The devastation to the fish and wildlife in the area could only be immense.

We caught seven of eight cartel growers, and no one fired a shot on either side. We MET guys pray for this resolution on every mission.

Just like in the first camp, this one had loaded handguns close to every bunk. We recovered a 12-gauge shotgun in the kitchen. With Shang, Tony and Mak maintaining security on the four additional suspects, Rumble and Phebe, Markos, Frog and I hiked through the final few trails in the grow. We found several more water diversions and countless more dead animals within the area. Satisfied we caught every grower possible, Shang called Jeffe at the command post and gave him the green light to send in the eradication and reclamation teams.

Future MET Delta Team snipers working hard during Santa Clara County sniper school training. Sniper-led observation teams would ultimately prove critical during surveillance operations used to take down cartel operations throughout the state.

Those teams came equipped with the necessary protection gear (nitrile gloves, long sleeves and exposure masks). Once inside, they started the long and arduous task of chopping down 20,000 poisoned marijuana plants and cleaning up the massive infrastructure throughout the sites. They needed to not only rectify the water diversions from the San Joaquin River and restore flow where needed, but also restore the site back to its natural state.

Our landing zone (LZ) was in a large agricultural field suited for helicopter eradication and reclamation operations. As case agent, Shang conducted interviews on all seven suspects back at the LZ and prepared them for transport to jail. Medical personnel who were staged in the LZ treated team members or suspects for injuries. They also made sure we stayed hydrated, as the temperature by mid-afternoon rose to well over 100 degrees.

Several patrol division game wardens also stood by in the LZ, ready to transport the suspects to jail. The reclamation and marijuana trailers, as well as helicopter support crews, readied to handle the numerous net loads of weed and grow waste that would be coming out shortly.

On the shaded side of the LZ, the FOX News crew waited for an update and overview of the mission. They collected my interior grow complex footage and later combined it with their interviews, helicopter overflight shots and environmental commentary related to the drought. In the end, they produced a comprehensive, informative and alarming story. Their focus on all the environmental issues — especially the cartel's widespread use of banned Carbofuran-based poisons — made the story one of the most educational and beneficial ever for our MET. We still use it all over California and in other parts of the country to expose the hidden environmental and public safety wars that teams like ours fight daily.

The shock of seeing a full team of silent, camouflaged and heavily armed spec ops warriors surrounding them deflated the growers' will to fight. They gave up instantly. Their surrender was surreal ...

After 18 hours of nonstop operations, we wrapped up the Crows Landing Mission at sunset. Stanislaus's helicopter removed 18 huge net loads before dark. That capped off one of the largest complexes the MET ever worked. The Crows Landing operation resulted in the destruction of 20,000 poisoned marijuana plants, with a black-market street value of approximately $36 million. During the mission, we captured seven of the eight cartel growers and removed countless tons of waste, irrigation pipe, fertilizers and other environmentally damaging products. Given the drought conditions at the time of the operation, we saved 18 million gallons of much-needed San Joaquin River water from being stolen by the growers. Our team still debriefs the Crows Landing operation. We reflect on the challenges it presented, due to its size and location. The operation also made a great opportunity to hone our tactics. Although we identified key equipment and training needs during that op, it's the lifelong memories from events shared with teammates during the mission that will always be cherished.

I smile every time I think of crossing that deep slough with my brothers in the middle of the night under the green glow of our NVGs. We felt more alive than ever as we trudged through that dark, cold water. I'm exhilarated when reliving the chaos and chase we engaged in at the first camp, and at the memory of Phebe rocketing through the grass to capture fleeing suspects. I'm proud of my colleagues when I remember every twist and turn that mission threw at us, and the fill-and-flow mentality we all maintained for safety that day. In typical MET fashion, we adapted to make the mission a success, with everyone on the team pitching in where needed. ✹

N 90 22' 368"
W 123 93' 940"

CHAPTER 06

DELTA TEAM: CDFW'S FIRST SNIPER ELEMENT HITS THE GROUND RUNNING

"I am a sheepdog. I live to protect the flock and confront the wolf."

— Lt. Col. (ret.) Dave Grossman

SUMMER 2017 – REDWOOD FOREST – HUMBOLDT COUNTY, CALIFORNIA

Gene popped his Bobcat into gear and gunned the throttle, spilling several pounds of fresh potting soil from the tractor's half-raised front bucket as the vehicle lunged toward the big greenhouse. His co-op property was large and concealed, far off the beaten path and well away from any paved road, making law enforcement detection and infiltration almost impossible.

Even with another 10 growers working with him around the clock, Gene's crew fell behind the curve. Well into the 2017 cannabis season, with plenty of room in their massive greenhouse to facilitate another 4,000 plants, Gene knew they lost big money ($14 million, conservatively) by not having these plants in the ground. This pissed him off, and he continued to work to remedy the deficit.

Another thought frustrated Gene: a memory from less than 12 months ago, when recklessness cost him. He and his young buddy, Wheels, illegally

A MET Delta Team sniper ranges targets from his final firing position (FFP).

spotlighted deer and other animals in the Carlotta area of Humboldt County. The killers poached this remote region for years without any problems until that night. Gene remained baffled by how a game warden knew where they would be committing their wildlife crimes on that night. The officer, waiting from a hidden truck, surprised the two men red-handed just after midnight. Gene and Wheels had been caught flat-footed while shining their light over the surrounding forest and carrying guns in the truck. The warden lit them up like a Christmas tree with bright red and blue lights and a siren.

Gene relived their split-second decision to run for it that night and open fire on the game warden during the chase. They'd been on the run ever since. He regretted not taking out the wildlife officer, because dead men tell no tales. Looking over his shoulder 24/7 sucked, as he knew the entire Humboldt County law enforcement community had its eyes peeled for him.

At least at the complex on this mountain, far from town and law enforcement, Gene felt safe. No one could sneak up on his complex.

Or so he thought.

Across the canyon 250 yards away, Markos lay motionless in his well-camouflaged hide, invisible to even the trained eye. He tracked Gene through his sniper rifle's optics, placing the scope reticle ahead of the Bobcat. He recorded every detail about the man operating it. Gene's facial features displayed crystal clear, even under the long, late-afternoon shadows covering the ground around the greenhouse.

Lying prone in near darkness, with the sun at his back and behind three layers of brush and timber, Markos grinned as he confirmed Gene's identity. Along with the rest of Delta Team positioned around the greenhouse complex, the designated marksman/observer (DMO) had waited for this moment for 48 hours — a relief for Markos, now in the middle of a three-day fugitive identification and recovery mission. Observing, documenting and coordinating the capture of Gene formed the critical first steps in an allied-agency plan to apprehend the poacher. Markos' visual confirmation of Gene's presence at the complex turned the wheels of justice into motion and changed the life of this outlaw forever.

16 YEARS EARLIER - SANTA CLARA - APRIL 2001

Proned out on the sniper pad, Markos and I sat shoulder to shoulder, surrounded by a diverse mix of law enforcement and military snipers from all over the West Coast. Just six months before the 9/11 terrorist attacks, we didn't know how relevant and pivotal this — and many other tactical classes — would be for our careers and the future tactical developments within our agency.

In the middle of the third day of a 50-hour basic sniper school run by the Santa Clara County Sheriff's Office, we conducted 200-yard command-fire drills with the entire class of 16 precision riflemen. Command fire involved two or more snipers firing simultaneously to handle multiple threats. We used this technique when there are multiple exposed targets, or when targets positioned behind solid barriers must be penetrated for the critical shot to be accurate and effective. Useful for hostage scenarios or deadly force threats behind glass barriers, it required a combination of concentration, coordination and precise trigger mechanics. Every sniper on gun must be in sync with the team leader calling the shot. When executed correctly, it sounds impressive, like an artillery boom from a single rifle.

SEAL Team snipers used command fire during the Maersk Alabama hijacking incident in 2009 to engage three armed Somali pirates holding Captain Phillips hostage. The SEALS did so perfectly, and Phillips survived that horrific incident — a testament to the technique and the team's training and expertise.

Our division didn't have a tactical-entry or a sniper team at the time, so Markos and I took the class on our own time and expense. It would surely improve our operations on the environmental crime front.

When working poaching cases together, Markos and I always gravitated to the remote backcountry poaching details, far away from roads. We preferred digging in deep to catch untouchable, righteous poachers who baited and killed deer illegally. We set up surveillance hides — sometimes for as long as two months — to catch a group of poachers. Watching the ripple effect within the poaching community following a takedown engendered the most rewarding feeling. By using fieldcraft and sniper tactics, we caught the ones who mattered — poachers so embedded and comfortable in their killing that they needed to be caught red-handed and taken out of circulation indefinitely.

Much like the effect a sniper has on the battlefield, these operations demoralized even the most insulated wildlife criminals. Although we lacked precision rifles and optics, Markos, myself and many other game wardens executed surveillance details for years that were otherwise like sniper team deployments.

Although the CDFW's Law Enforcement Division was a long way from having a much-needed comprehensive tactical unit, I knew we would need these skills — and many more — to build this team. When our leadership eventually developed a spec ops team to combat the more challenging wildlife-resource threats, a handful of us would already have the right skill set to make it happen.

Six months prior to the class, Markos and I bought and built our own sniper rifles — a pair of Remington Police Sniper System (PSS) rifles. We couldn't afford a more expensive rifle system, such as those issued to some other agency snipers. We topped them with Leupold Mark IV 3-10X tactical scopes with mil-dot reticles. We also purchased 1,000 rounds of Remington 168-grain match-grade ammunition for each of us. We zeroed our rifles at 100 yards for the upcoming school. After getting velocity averages for both rifles, I developed individual dope cards. Even though we would not shoot past 300 yards in sniper school, we confirmed solid dope out to 800 yards for both rifles in the event we ever had to make a long-range shot.

Through the winter of 2001, Markos and I spent countless hours on a friend's ranch in the Silicon Valley foothills training with our new precision rifles. The accuracy and consistency of the PSS system impressed us. The rifles maintained 0.5 MOA five-shot groups at 100 yards if we did our part on the bench or prone. It performed well under the 1.0 MOA standard required for the upcoming school.

Our rifles matched or exceeded the accuracy levels of more expensive and elaborate rifle systems in sniper school. We realized it's the operator — not the rifle system and gadgets — that makes the system most effective. Our game warden backgrounds fit in well for the class. We already experienced hundreds of weapon systems, stalking, hide building and long-range surveillance. The light bulb went off when we realized that game warden field tactics and sniper training are synonymous.

Over the next few years, Markos and I enrolled into every available tactical school hosted by an agency with a Tier 1 SWAT unit. We gained statewide acceptance from military and law enforcement special operations personnel, and we jumped at every opportunity to learn from these highly skilled professionals.

Spag was promoted to team leader of his sniper unit during this time and took Sierra Team's training and capabilities to the next level. As veterans

Sniper school instructors (from left): Rails, Snake, Apache, K9 Jordan, the author, Spag and One Shot.

of his agency's basic sniper school, we knew how it could be expanded and improved upon. Sierra One reached out to me in 2009 to assist him in improving the basic sniper school. I jumped at the chance, but we agreed we couldn't stop there.

Given the rural, wooded environment Spag's team and our game wardens worked in most of the time, we identified a significant training void for law enforcement snipers nationwide. The time was overdue for an advanced sniper school that focused on more complicated topics (long-distance shooting, high-angle shots, effects of rifle canting, long-range low-light shooting, after-dark shooting with NVGs, long-distance cross-country stalking, mil-dot use and distance calculations, wind drift and leads, long-distance moving-target engagement, shooting from and within vehicles, urban and rural hide building, etc.). This advanced class needed a lot of work to develop and host, but the benefits to allied-agency and military snipers all over the West Coast would be well worth it.

For the next six months, we revamped the basic school, including rewriting

This is what a typical DTO trespass marijuana grow plot looks like. This picture was taken at Bodfish Creek in 2012.

One container of EPA-banned Metafos poison, such as this one recovered at a DTO trespass grow site, can kill as many as 2,500 people. If it seeps into water, it will kill any animal stopping by for a drink.

Mexican cartels often use Panga boats, such as this one, to smuggle goods. Authorities found this one abandoned along the California coastline with 6,000 pounds of processed black-market marijuana ready for sale in the United States.

MET operators seized this fully automatic AK-47 at a grow site. Cartel growers make no distinction between law enforcement and everyday civilians out for a hike. They'll protect their crop at any cost.

MET operators engage in a physical training drill — a team-building log run for cardiovascular and strength endurance. Because of the long hours and distances, operators must be in top condition. The days of Barney Fife-style game wardens are long gone.

K9 Phebe is pictured here with MET operators during the 2012 Croy Road operation. Like many other K9s, cancer ended Phebe's long run of dedicated service. It's believed that the noxious chemicals found at grow sites contribute to K9 health risks.

Cartel water-diversion pumps like this one steal thousands of gallons of California Delta water per day. With record-breaking droughts hitting California like never before, the consequences reach far into all parts of the state's economy.

Cartel narco-traffickers worship patron saints as a way to sanction their violence and launder their guilt. As such, shrines like this one are a common sight at illegal grows. This quasi-religion plugs neatly into the Catholic background in Mexico, where most growers originate, even if it requires perverting existing saints or inventing new ones.

Cartel growers select public wildlands for their operations because of the seclusion. Law enforcement tactics must evolve to match any remote scenario. Here, MET horses deploy in a sensitive wilderness area where no motor vehicles are allowed.

Working with CDFW's offshore patrol boat fleet for homeland security, Panga boat interdiction and vessel-entry training.

After a raid comes "reclamation." That involves reversing the environmental impacts of a grow site, such as this diversion set up along an endangered steelhead trout stream.

A cartel grower poses with a poisoned golden eagle near his trespass marijuana plants. All you need to know about these growers' concern for wildlife can be summed up in this single picture.

Bags of processed cartel marijuana for pending sale. Often tainted with EPA-banned poisons, this bud is sold throughout the country to unknowing consumers.

The Patriot Ordnance Factory (POF) P308 carbine was a game-changer for the Marijuana Enforcement Team's load-out. The carbines are chambered in the hard-hitting, wall-penetrating 7.62 NATO (.308 Win.) cartridge and are much shorter and handier to carry through thick brush than were the long, heavy M14s the team previously carried.

This Pave Hawk helicopter, operated by the California Air National Guard's (CANG) counter-drug task force, takes part in Operation PRISTINE. Helicopter support is crucial to success, but it comes with a significant price tag. Without funding, this bird would be grounded. That's a major challenge in states facing a budget crunch.

An AK-47-armed cartel grower poses in a national forest. This type of public safety threat keeps people at home, away from public wildlands. Fewer people using the land legally could equal a funding shortage later. This issue isn't only about marijuana. It's bigger than that.

The author puts the new lightweight 7.62 NATO POF308 AR Revolution carbine through its paces during MET range training.

K9 Phebe sits at the steps of the California State Capitol during Senate and Assembly MET and K9 resolution ceremonies in January 2017. Known as the Fur Missile, Phebe proved vital on missions and also for educating lawmakers.

Carbofuran, a poison used at cartel marijuana grow sites, killed this gray fox. When audiences sympathetic to cannabis use and skeptical of law enforcement see photos like this one, their opinions about MET operations quickly change. The problem of illegal grows includes the cannabis issue, but it's not limited to it.

A MET sniper uses an ATV for backcountry recon.

The P308 carbine from Patriot Ordnance Factory, custom engraved with the California Department of Fish and Game warden badge. It's equipped with the Aimpoint H-1 red-dot sight for fast target acquisition against gun-wielding cartel combatants encountered during raids.

MET operators conduct offshore small-vessel deadly force threat-engagement training. Many cartels circumvent the U.S.-Mexico border with boats.

MET operators, command staff and K9 Phebe stop for a picture with lawmakers and civilians on the California Senate floor during a resolution ceremony in January 2017. No matter their politics, lawmakers agreed that the threats posed by illegal growers must be stopped.

A MET operator conducts high-altitude rappel training in the eastern Sierra Nevada Mountains.

Shang examines the depth of a well dug for black-market marijuana cultivation.

It's not a day at the beach. MET operator physical training includes swimming with K9s.

Delta Team operators move into position during sniper school stalking exercises.

California Air National Guard's Counter-Drug Task Force Pave Hawk helicopter removes a load of marijuana and grow site waste.

MET operators travel by horseback during an operation in a high-altitude wilderness area. Horses produce less noise than ATVs, making them ideal for long treks.

The MET Delta Team uses modular and compact POF Designated Marksman Rifles (DMR). The smaller size is better suited to fieldwork.

Illegal growers often use EPA-banned poisons to wipe out wildlife around their plots. These black bears are only a few of the tragic examples. If these poisons can do this to bears, imagine what they can do to the people buying and smoking the illegal weed.

A fully equipped special operations MET, ready to deploy anywhere, day or night.

The author (left) runs accuracy drills with future MET Delta Team snipers at the Santa Clara County sniper school in 2011.

the instructor and student manuals. By mid-summer, we hosted our first allied-agency basic sniper school in October 2009. Along with Spag and myself, MET veterans and fellow snipers Snake, Rails, Apache and One Shot helped instruct the 50-hour school. With a solid, challenging curriculum taught by motivated, experienced instructors, a long waiting list of allied-agency operators stretched from all over the West Coast for our next class.

Over the winter of 2009–'10, Spag, myself and the rest of Sierra Team wrote the manual for the advanced class and planned the curriculum. The first advanced class filled to capacity and has every year since.

In spring of 2011 — well before the CDFW MET unit was developed — I brought Shang and Markos to Santa Clara County to attend basic sniper school. Although both operators benefitted immensely from training, we also needed to test our POF P308 carbines in a precision-shooting setting.

With the Rock 5R barrel serving as the backbone of the POF platform, we knew from benchrest testing that the short-barreled patrol carbines were

Shang stalks into position during Delta Team sniper training.

accurate. But were they accurate enough to pass sniper school standards, function reliably and keep up with the accurized, match-grade bolt-action guns that dominated the class? Curious, we replaced the Aimpoint H-1 red-dot sights on the patrol carbines with Leupold Mark IV 4.5-14x50 TMR illuminated-reticle tactical scopes.

With no other changes to their patrol carbines, Markos and Shang excelled during the course, completing all drills successfully with the accuracy standard needed to pass the class. Although the P308 carbines proved not quite as accurate as the bolt-action rifles in the course, they shot close to the required 1 MOA accuracy standard — good enough for a short-barreled, lightweight gun capable of mobility and rapid follow-up shots.

With Markos and Shang certified as snipers, we added two more precision riflemen within our ranks. That brought the total to four, counting myself and Frog's SEAL team background. We formed the first CDFW LED sniper team in history.

DEC. 17, 2013 - SANTA CLARA COUNTY SHERIFF'S RANGE

Special Operations Assistant Chief Rumble asked Nate and I what we required to develop a sniper team under the MET umbrella. Rumble needed to convince the chief that a sniper team could make a difference in our operations. It was music to my ears. For more than a decade up to that point, I pushed for our agency to sanction such a team. Like Nate, Rumble saw the need for snipers within our spec ops umbrella. The time finally came on the same day we solidified full-time positions for our agency's first dedicated MET tactical unit.

The previous summer of dangerous backcountry MET missions justified the move. Snipers could have gathered critical information during long-range surveillance and/or provided a safety blanket on overwatch for our grow site entry team below. Besides our own operations, a MET sniper team could assist other high-risk indoor entry units on operations and provide support during homeland security or crisis events. Besides, the warden force already used agency-approved, easily convertible POF rifles.

Given the green light, we embraced the challenge of developing our agency's first sniper unit, Delta Team, shortly after the new year. Delta Team was comprised of a designated marksman/observer (DMO) unit capable of deploying at any time and anywhere for surveillance, reconnaissance, precision rifle and other unique missions. After analyzing several federal, state and county sniper program policies, we crafted a DMO policy consistent with our LED's use-of-force policy that allowed us to integrate with allied agencies on any mutual aid mission.

We stuck with our POF P308s because our agency wasn't in a financial position to procure new rifle systems for our team. Fortunately, we already proved the compact carbines could do the job. Although we considered longer-barreled upper receivers, we decided to stick with our 16-inch barrels with flash-hiders for maneuverability and weight savings. Not a featherweight by any means, our platform with optics, sling, bipod and other accessories still weighed lighter than longer-barreled sniper rifles. The compact size fit in well with missions that required long-distance stalks — sometimes at high elevation — and always over rough, densely vegetated terrain.

Just like our carbines, our DMO rifles were painted in olive drab and outfitted with Flat Dark Earth furniture for natural camouflage. For optics, we stuck with the Leupold Mark IV 4.5-14x50 tactical scope with an illuminated TMR reticle. This rugged, compact scope handled any shot we needed to make.

For engaging threats at close range, such as during raids, we added a LaRue 45-degree mount to the scope and topped it with an Aimpoint H-1 Micro red-dot sight. This setup also allowed us to engage threats beyond 600 yards if necessary. The compact rifle can make reliable headshots beyond 200 yards and torso shots past 600 yards — the outer limit of engagements we encountered during MET operations.

Like our MET, Delta Team often operated in the dark, and we needed a compact, lightweight night vision optic (NVO) suited to the rifle. After testing several NVOs, we chose the Night Optics D950 Generation III Starlight. Light, small, and easy to use, the D950 allowed us to make critical observations under magnification during surveillance operations and on suspect-identification missions after dark.

We established stringent monthly training and quarterly qualification standards for Delta Team. We trained at elevations ranging from sea level to above 11,000 feet in the eastern Sierra Nevada Mountains. We required standing, kneeling, sitting and prone shooting positions on shots ranging from 50 to 200 yards. Running more than 200 yards during the course simulated the heart rate of actual engagements under stress.

We also tested in complete darkness while navigating uneven terrain with only the NVOs on the DMO rifles and helmet-mounted NVG systems. This afforded us maximum stealth and increased officer safety, allowing us to move and shoot with pinpoint accuracy at night, when most of Delta Team's deployments took place.

With the DMO program operational by the spring of 2014, we built and broke in our rifle systems and set up our kits. The new sniper unit comprised of six people from all over the state (Frog, Markos, Shang, Quinn, Mak and me).

Delta Team operators during high-altitude rappel training in California's eastern Sierra range.

In April, I ran Delta Team through the revamped basic sniper school to freshen up everyone's training and give the new rifles a solid field test. The guys did great, showing that the compact guns could do the job.

In the fall of 2014, we hosted another advanced sniper school, with Delta Team in attendance. By the end of 2014, Delta Team's first operational year, the team completed both schools and deployed several times on DMO missions to support MET operations throughout the state.

JULY 2014 – SANTA CRUZ MOUNTAINS – SANTA CRUZ COUNTY, CALIFORNIA

Delta Team deployed for the first time on a CDFW-run multi-team operation in the mountains east of Santa Cruz for an illegal private-land marijuana grow.

The suspects not only grew marijuana illegally on their property, but also trespassed onto Santa Cruz County open space to grow their crop. The growers diverted and polluted a small tributary to Soquel Creek, affecting one of the few remaining anadromous fish waters left on the North Coast. We later learned the suspects also operated a concentrated-cannabis, butane honey oil (BHO) lab, adding to the felony violations on the property.

We needed a big team. The grow sites and BHO lab sat close to the suspects' two dwellings. We created a straightforward plan: Our Delta Bay Enhanced Enforcement Program (DBEEP) unit would handle the high-risk entry of the main house, while a complement of MET operators would hit a smaller cabin approximately 100 yards from the house. Both entries needed to happen simultaneously to protect officers, catch the suspects by surprise and ensure evidence, illegal weapons or other contraband was not disposed of during the raid.

Nate and I agreed to utilize Delta Team to support both entry teams. Our agency had yet to utilize snipers on an operation, and the scenario presented an ideal opportunity. Markos, Frog, Shang and I deployed.

Delta Team's mission was to move into hide positions on the backside of the houses and provide pre-raid surveillance and overwatch security for our entry teams when they hit the houses after first light. This proved more complicated than expected. The woods surrounding the target structures grew thick. We ran into snags in several spots en route to our hide locations, including hidden live-in structures full of people and watchdogs. This forced us to take circuitous routes to avoid being compromised.

Markos took point with me, with Frog and Shang following behind. We tried to remain as quiet as possible in the noisy woods. It took us more than an hour longer than planned to get into position, but we set up just in time to be effective.

Shang and Frog covered the cabin, while Markos and I oversaw the house. When the entry teams hit both structures an hour later, we covered the back doors in case a suspect ran out or, worse, brandished a weapon during the

Markos during Delta Team's high-altitude accuracy drills and ballistic testing at 11,000 feet in California's eastern Sierra Nevada Mountains.

The author (left) and Shang scan the area during a Delta Team deployment at high altitude.

warrant service. Knowing ahead of time what our entry teams were walking into was a godsend and a security blanket.

That first deployment illustrated the necessity of Delta Team's addition to the MET. As of this writing, Delta Team has operated for five years and worked in almost every part of the state. Our diverse missions have included after-dark NVG surveillance on cartel growers destroying the flatlands of the Central Valley, and hiking glacial mountains at elevations of more than 10,000-feet elevation to protect endangered Sierra Nevada bighorn sheep from DTO grow operations.

Delta Team's most significant deployment to date involved confirmation of Gene's presence at that greenhouse-cultivation operation in Humboldt County in 2017. Markos made that critical observation, accompanied by three Delta Team operators embedded in the woods for the operation. Our team hiked cross-country over rough, steep, densely wooded terrain in complete darkness to set up hides on the complex and wait to identify and/or capture the fugitive. Unsupported and on their guns for more than 72 hours, Delta Team members did not leave the mountain until the mission completed.

After being on the run for almost a year, Gene went into custody within two weeks of our team confirming his presence at the greenhouse complex. Besides a large allied-agency effort to locate and capture him, numerous donors — including the California Wildlife Officers Foundation (CWOF) and California Fish and Game Warden Supervisors and Managers Association (CFGWSMA) — sponsored a reward program to aid the apprehension mission.

On Jan. 16, 2018, a court convicted Gene of numerous felonies, including assault with a firearm on a peace officer (with an enhancement of personally using a firearm), being a felon in possession of a firearm, using threats and violence upon an executive officer and negligently discharging a firearm at an occupied vehicle. Much to our satisfaction, Gene was also convicted of spotlighting (using an artificial light to poach wildlife at night), a single but important misdemeanor because of the shooting assault of one of our game wardens.

Through our missions, Delta Team validated several key program designs that apply to all snipers operating in similar environments. The more compact and lightweight our DMO rifle system, the more effective the team can perform. We validated this fact countless times during sniper training and team deployments in hot, densely wooded terrain and the long distances we often hike with our DMO rifle kits. Delta's 2017 missions proved to us that smaller and lighter are sometimes better. 🌿

N 38 19' 415"
W 121 40' 544"

CHAPTER 07

LIBERTY ISLAND: K9 OPS AND PATRON SAINTS ON THE SACRAMENTO DELTA

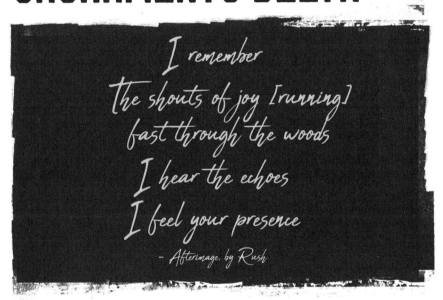

I remember
the shouts of joy [running]
fast through the woods
I hear the echoes
I feel your presence

— Afterimage, by Rush

JULY 2016 – LIBERTY ISLAND SLOUGH SYSTEM – SACRAMENTO DELTA

Parked in one of his favorite lookouts along Shag Slough, Tony sat on the tailgate of his pickup truck, eating lunch and watching small boats full of fishermen drift by. He knew this area of the Delta well. For the better part of a decade, Tony and his DBEEP teammates focused on the poaching of the Delta's striped bass, sturgeon and sturgeon roe, all hot commodities for organized crime groups. The game changed recently when another, even more dangerous environmental criminal infiltrated the Delta: the Mexican drug cartels.

Shortly after Marijuana Enforcement Team's development in 2013, a surge of drug trafficking organization cultivation operations popped up in the Sacramento Delta. From 2013 to 2016, at the peak of California's historic drought, we noticed a shift in DTO activity away from the mountains to the flatlands, primarily around the Sacramento Delta. With some mountain streams completely dry for the first time in decades, some historic water sources were no longer available for cultivation. Cartel growers found an ideal new base of operations during the drought in the Delta's 1,100 square miles of densely vegetated waterways.

Usually, during low- and high-tide cycles, Tony found good luck in this spot. Over the years, he identified numerous vessels associated with wildlife crimes and made good poaching cases as a result. He crossed his fingers, but wasn't optimistic. The weather was hot, and only a handful of the most die-hard fishermen had passed by in the last hour.

With his lunch finished, Tony bagged his food wrappers and closed the tailgate before walking to the front of the truck. He opened the driver's door and paused before stepping into the driver's seat. He looked back at the water one last time and focused on the dark current of Shag Slough. Tony couldn't take his eyes off the water. His warden's intuition kicked in. He couldn't explain why, but he knew he needed to stay. Thirty seconds passed, then a minute, and still nothing. Frustrated and ready to give up, Tony started to climb into the driver's seat when he saw it.

A small, well-used, flat-bottomed fishing boat with two men on board and a couple of fishing rods leaning over the skiff's edge drifted with the tide. At first glance, these men fit the profile of dedicated Delta fisherman, but something looked off. They were not dressed right to be fishermen, and the brand-new flotation vest one man wore seemed out of place.

Tony couldn't lock down exactly what these guys were up to, but DTO marijuana cultivation came to mind. Our MET previously teamed up with DBEEP to take down a cartel grow close to this area. These "fishermen" headed in that same direction. Tony suspected these guys could be cartel growers or supply crew for a grow operation. He waited for the skiff to pass out of view before jumping into his truck and heading back to town.

Tony called me shortly after spotting the boat, and I shared his excitement upon hearing his story. I agreed we needed to start an investigation immediately and bring MET and DBEEP together for another Delta-based DTO case if warranted. We needed to first verify that these guys were indeed part of a grow operation. If so, we needed to identify the players involved and learn the grow site locations and routes of travel before we could develop a takedown plan. We wasted no time in beginning the process.

Tony coordinated surveillance operations for DBEEP, with our MET operators assisting. Over the next four weeks, we locked down the location of two active DTO trespass grow sites on Liberty Island near Shag Slough. One proved relatively small, but the second one was a big live-in complex. We also connected the two "fishermen" to both cultivation sites. They handled day-to-day operations along with several other operatives.

Tony and his DBEEP teammates focused on the poaching of the Delta's striped bass, sturgeon and sturgeon roe, all hot commodities for organized crime groups. The game changed recently when another, even more dangerous environmental criminal infiltrated the Delta: the Mexican drug cartels.

The narrow, shallow waterway of Shag Slough, even at high tide, made mission planning challenging. We needed to coordinate our entry with the tide to make it to both grow sites. The only way to infiltrate the sites without detection was by boat. The wide expanse of the Delta's waterways played to our advantage.

Given the terrain and the distance between grow sites, we needed a big team for the operation. Even with team members from both MET and DBEEP, we still lacked enough personnel to pull it off. Luckily, Long (my firearms committee training partner for the POF carbine transition program), brought his whole squad to assist from Northern California Delta Region. With Long's help, we roped in more than 20 operators and logistics personnel, giving us enough officers to fill three separate entry teams.

By land or by water. Rumble and K9 Phebe use a kayak for exfiltration from the Liberty Island grow complex, following apprehension, eradication and reclamation operations.

HIDDEN WAR

We dedicated two entry teams to the bigger live-in grow, with both teams traveling by water using DBEEP's state-of-the-art patrol boats. Brian — a squad mate from my district patrol days on the Central Coast and a skilled DBEEP vessel operator — would run our big jet boat shuttle. After an hour-long jet boat insertion during the middle of the night to the edge of the slough, half of the team would offload and navigate the rest of the way to the grow site using kayaks, an exciting caveat to this mission. Using kayaks for our final entry were Tony, Mattos (Tony's DBEEP teammate), Frog, myself and Rumble and K9 Phebe. Most of us kayaked for daylight water patrols before, but this marked the first time any of us used them on a stealth entry into a DTO grow operation. We didn't know how K9 Phebe would handle the ride, given this would be her first time in a kayak.

I led the kayak operators, while Quinn ran team leader for the second half of Team One's entry element. His team would drop off farther down on the bank of Shag Slough, following our kayak team's departure. Quinn would lead his team's stalk on foot the rest of the way to the grow complex. The plan allowed us to stalk toward the grow from both sides. We'd create a choke point in the middle and tighten the apprehension noose on anyone inside. Plus, with Rumble and K9 Phebe on my team, and DBEEP operator Tom and his K9 Luna on Quinn's, we carried sufficient K9 support.

Team Two would handle the second grow site, located about a mile from the live-in complex. Raid timing proved critical because both grows likely stayed in communication with each other. With good cell coverage in the region, we couldn't risk being compromised by one grower calling another when our teams made contact.

Team Two would parallel our hour-long ride through the Delta to Liberty Island before breaking off to another drop-off point near the slough. Sean — a skilled boat operator from Long's patrol squad — ran that vessel. A fellow lieutenant/DBEEP supervisor and three operators from his team came along. Tango from our MET was also present, along with Pat and K9 Karma — another K9 team from Long's patrol squad. We felt fortunate to have a K9 on all three entry teams — a rare luxury.

AUGUST 2016 - LIBERTY ISLAND - SACRAMENTO DELTA

Sitting next to Rumble and Frog on the stern of DBEEP's jet boat, I faced our

MET and DBEEP operators paddle kayaks to access the Liberty Island DTO trespass grow complex.

wake and the swirling Delta waters behind us in the pre-dawn darkness. Phebe dozed at our feet, her head resting on Rumble's boot. She saved her energy for when she would need it most.

Another half-hour of high-speed boat travel stretched out ahead of us. After that, we'd transition to silence in the kayaks. Just past the end of our wake, I could barely make out the silhouette of our second jet boat, matching our speed and paralleling our course. We took the time to rest and mentally prepare for what was ahead.

Frog tapped my shoulder and held up two fingers, indicating we were two minutes from the drop. A minute later, Brian cut the boat's throttle and we drifted with the current in silence the rest of the way toward the bank of Shag Slough. We offloaded the kayaks, dropping the noisy polymer boats into the water as quietly as possible.

One of several non-game birds killed by highly toxic poisons used by marijuana growers in the Liberty Island site. Wildlife destruction around grow sites is widespread and indiscriminate. Sights like this one make game wardens furious.

With enough ambient light to see terrain features and navigate safely, we loaded our kit gear and weapons and settled into our individual boats. With everyone in the stack ready to roll, we began the two-mile paddle. On point, Tony led us up the river, paddling quickly against the outgoing tide. Mattos and Frog followed behind, with Rumble and Phebe to the rear of them. I followed Rumble and the Fur Missile in the tail position, looking over my shoulder routinely to check our six. Phebe looked stoic on the bow of Rumble's kayak, her ears perked up and nose working overtime, trying to sniff out suspects, marijuana, firearms or any other grow indicators.

After 30 minutes of hard paddling, we turned into a small tributary. Tony had

Shrines to patron saints are common to DTO grow complexes linked to cartels.

done his homework to find this one from the thousands of narrow channels spider-webbing around Liberty Island. In slack current, with every noise amplified, we paddled with slow and careful movements, cringing at the noises made by the overhanging branches as they scratched against our kayaks. As we closed in on the grow site, the channel closed in on us. The slough's banks stood only a few feet on either side of us. Crossing under and through willow tree and blackberry branches that spanned the channel, we moved at a snail's pace to stay silent.

Minutes later, Phebe sniffed the air and paced the bow of Rumble's kayak. She smelled suspects. Twenty yards farther, Phebe alerted again, even more excited this time. Rumble signaled that he heard voices ahead. We stopped to listen, even though we were still a quarter-mile from the last known location of the suspect boat. Two men spoke softly in Spanish not more than 25 to 30 yards away. Only a thick wall of vegetation along the slough's bank separated us.

In front of us stood thousands of 3-foot-tall marijuana plants in irrigation holes. We found ourselves positioned well south of the growers we heard earlier. With the other half of our team stalking in from the north, we could pin down the growers.

We needed to gain some distance from the suspects. One at a time, barely clearing the banks of the channel, we turned the kayaks around and moved away from the grow. On point now, I led us 100 yards from the voices.

With the sun rising, and the chance of being spotted increasing, we climbed out of our kayaks. We pushed across the muddy bottom, submersed up to our waists, straight into a wall of tules, cattails, thorny blackberry bushes and willow branches. Tony and Frog hit the wall first. When I asked how it looked, Frog rolled his eyes and said, "None of it looks good, bro. We need to find another way."

Within minutes, we circumvented the riparian barrier and ended up in a perfect spot: the southern edge of the grow site. In front of us stood thousands of 3-foot-tall marijuana plants in irrigation holes. We found ourselves positioned well south of the growers we heard earlier. With the other half of our team stalking in from the north, we could pin down the growers.

Even with both elements of Team One in perfect position on both sides of the suspects, we still had a lot of terrain to cover without being compromised.

Because contact with the targets could happen at any second, we did the Montana Two-Step. This meant hunting along the edge of the growers' main access trail, stalking and stopping after a few steps to look and listen. After 30 minutes, we found their camp and kitchen complex, and a makeshift boat dock concealed along the edge of another hidden tributary to the slough. The main trail led through the living area. Thick vegetation obscured the trail from aerial observation. Next to the dock sat a gas-powered water pump, with its source hose plunged into slough water. A concealed grass landing hid two, small motor-powered skiffs, including the one Tony spotted more than a month earlier. A sheen of gas and oil pooled up next to the skiffs, polluting the water.

> We've even recovered a written bible honoring the saint and her teachings (*Biblia de la Santa Muerte*). The *Los Zetas* and *El Gulfo* cartel factions worshipped this new folk saint, as did many other narco-trafficking gangs. Among their beliefs are ritual killing, offering of human body parts and cannibalism.

A wooden plank footbridge spanned the narrow waterway. We glided across it and took a knee along the edge of the camp. Several well-hidden branch bunks carved out of willow trees and brush clusters were scattered about the complex. We found sleeping bags, personal electronics, knives and various calibers of handgun and rifle ammunition in them.

The kitchen and a processing area for budded marijuana plants sat below the bunk area. Several hundred pounds of drying marijuana buds hung from thin wire lines above us, with another 25 pounds of thick, sticky buds stretched out on a thin mesh hammock below the drying lines. On a wooden platform rested digital scales and gallon-sized plastic storage bags. All of this told us the growers were efficient. They handled all phases of processing before their product left the site. They stashed thousands of pounds of fertilizer and other chemicals, including a few containers of banned and toxic Carbofuran throughout the camp as well.

As we cleared the rest of the camp, I noticed another cartel indicator. Just past the growers' bunks, in the brush at the base of a tree, a small tarp tied off to form an A-frame shrine. Several patron saint candles — half of them still burning — stood within the small structure. We find these shrines in a

A closeup of narco-traffickers' patron saint candles found in an outdoor DTO grow complex. The saints must have been on vacation the day this photo was taken by law enforcement.

majority of DTO outdoor grows, and we see more of them in grow sites, cartel stash houses and vehicles each year. These shrines and other patron saint paraphernalia can tell us a lot about a grow operation and those who run it.

Cartel operatives burned candles to pay homage to their saints. They also offered gifts (food, cigarettes, playing cards, wildflowers from near their grow site, etc.) within these shrines, believing they'd be blessed for success in their operations. Many figures worshiped by cartel groups are legitimate Roman Catholic saints (*San Ramon, Saint Jude, Nino de Atocha* and *Toribio Romo*). The cartels pervert the saints' sanctity to suit narco-trafficking cartel groups and justify their crimes. In this way, DTO crews operate similarly to extreme terrorist groups. Both believe their spiritual salvation sanctions — and even encourages — heinous acts of violence.

Candles burned to honor manufactured patron saints, such as *Santa Muerte* (Saint Death), *Saint Judas, Jesus Malverde* and *San Nazario* (the Craziest One) to supposedly insulate narco-traffickers from law enforcement. Shrines in DTO camp and kitchen complexes might contain numerous patron saint candle containers. We often found hundreds of unburned candles. Operatives in these complexes must ensure that their candles always burn day and night to keep them safe.

Because they sport the likenesses of the patron saints on their glass containers, the candles can clue us in to which cartel group is responsible for a specific grow. For instance, *La Familia Michoacana* (LFM) and the *Caballeros Templarios* (Knights Templar) cartels favored *San Nazario*. Their crimes played a direct role in the worship of this manufactured saint. According to their beliefs, worshiping "The Craziest One" required torture, ritual killing and cannibalism.

Along with bandits, outlaws and other drug traffickers, the Sinaloa Cartel worshipped *Jesus Malverde* — another unsanctioned saint known as a generous Robin Hood-like bandit. Narco-traffickers adored Malverde, and we saw signs of this patron saint in grow sites all over the country. We found wood carvings, necklaces, bracelets, candle containers, hats, clothing and belt buckles with his image in DTO trespass grow operations throughout the United States.

Even *Santa Muerte* (Saint Death) — a female grim reaper wearing a hooded cloak — attracted a strong criminal following all over Mexico. Along with Malverde, we saw Saint Muerte shrines within outdoor grow sites, on DTO vehicles and within stash houses. We've even recovered a written bible honoring the saint and her teachings (*Biblia de la Santa Muerte*). The *Los Zetas* and *El Gulfo* cartel factions worshipped this new folk saint, as did many other narco-trafficking gangs. Among their beliefs are ritual killing, offering of human body parts and cannibalism.

This brutal mindset lacked any regard for human life. It's difficult for many to understand. The belief that certain factions of people (specific cartel and terrorist groups) can be sanctioned to kill for sport and pleasure is unfathomable. Just like extreme terrorist groups such as the so-called Islamic State, *Los Zetas* members truly believe they do God's work while beheading someone. It goes without saying that this factored as a force-multiplier that law enforcement took seriously.

Back to the operation.

Kneeling in the jungle-like vegetation along the trail's edge, we had barely covered 100 yards over the last 45 minutes when the Fur Missile alerted. Phebe turned her head, focusing on the path ahead. Her ears perked up and her nose sniffed in overdrive. Contact seemed imminent. Tony, Frog, Mattos and I sat up in a sprinter's stance, ready to launch at the suspects to support our K9.

A minute later, two growers appeared, moving along the main trail. In silence, they stopped every few yards to look around and check on their plants. We could hardly hear them talking, even though they were only 25 yards away. Both wore camouflage clothing that blended in perfectly with the surrounding vegetation. They disappeared every time they stopped.

Rumble called our tempo and held us in place, letting our suspects get as close as possible. We saw knives on both of their belts as they moved through the brush. One man held a large set of pruning shears, while the other carried a 5-gallon bucket. Rumble saw pistol holsters on each man's hip. He whispered this information into his radio and told us Phebe's launch was close. Rumble announced and identified us seconds later, and all hell broke loose.

Both men fled down the trail as Rumble released the Fur Missile, giving her the command to apprehend. She darted through the vegetation and tackled the larger, younger man like a lightning strike. The shocked grower crashed to the ground. Before he could pull his knife or pistol, Rumble, Frog and I were on him, handcuffing and immobilizing him within seconds.

Another 15 yards down the trail, Tony and Mattos had their hands full with the smaller, much older suspect. This man was clearly the boss, and he was pissed off. He swung his bucket at Tony. Fighting the grower on the ground with Mattos' help, Tony subdued the man and placed him in handcuffs.

Shocked at the audacity of his suspect attacking him with a bucket, Tony gave us a puzzled look and said, "He attacked me with a bucket! A bucket! You guys believe that?" We laughed before I shrugged and said, "At least it wasn't the typical auto pistol or long blade, bro. First time for a bucket, though."

Over the next eight hours, Team One worked nonstop to log evidence throughout the grow complex. We eradicated the 7,000 large marijuana plants and reclamated the grow site, camp, kitchen, processing complex and boat dock. Team Two's site turned out to be small and devoid of suspects, so they joined us after eradicating and restoring their area. We worked the California Highway Patrol helicopter and its aircrew hard all day, pulling out several tons of trash, fertilizers, chemicals and black irrigation pipe.

We cleared the complex by late afternoon and were ready for some hydration and relaxation. Tango, Quinn and several other team members fired up the suspects' skiffs and used them for operator transport back to the DBEEP jet boat shuttles.

After the CHP helicopter hoisted the final net load of waste, our kayak entry team paddled back to the jet boat. Fighting a low tide, we barely made it through the narrow, shallow sections of the slough's tributary, portaging boats over sections too shallow to float.

Despite the long, exhausting day, we paddled with excitement after a successful and adventurous mission. Back on the bow of her kayak, with a Gatorade bottle in her mouth, Phebe looked like a happy puppy that had just retrieved her first tennis ball. The day marked Phebe's 114th bite apprehension of dangerous cartel growers during her amazing 11-year career, and another instance in which she saved us from a knife attack or gunfight. She remained unstoppable through attempted stabbings and shootings, and beatings with rocks, logs and more. It's a track record that's unheard of for a K9 working in the MET's arduous operating conditions for so many years. Unknown to us then, the Liberty Island operation would be one of the Fur Missile's final missions.

My satisfaction and pride dampened a bit as I realized we likely raided only a small portion of the trespass grows in the Delta. There stood too much prime, hidden terrain for cartel growers, and far too few of us to search them. However, my spirits lifted when I focused on the impact from the operation. Conservatively, we eradicated $16 million worth of illegal marijuana plants

MET and DBEEP operators eradicate thousands of poisoned marijuana plants during the Liberty Island mission. In an ironic twist, the same boats the growers used to garden these plants would later be employed to transport them away from the site as suspects.

— a significant financial loss for the DTO crew working the complex. More importantly, we rectified all of the environmental damage and kept millions of gallons of water from being stolen from the Delta.

Every single mission counted. Each operation that protected the public from injury or death, saved wildlife, wildlands and waterways, and kept the DTOs looking over their shoulders was a win. We needed to run this marathon to its end, chalking up as many victories as possible along the journey.

JULY 24, 2018 – SILICON VALLEY FOOTHILLS – SANTA CLARA COUNTY

Parked on top of a mountain overlooking Silicon Valley, I sat in my truck, scanning for DTO grow signs, when I received the most painful phone call of my career. Rumble sounded in tears and barely discernable as he told me Phebe wouldn't survive the day. The Fur Missile had been diagnosed with an incurable cancer a month earlier. We all dreaded this day.

We reflected on Phebe's amazing K9 career and the countless moments when she risked everything to keep us safe. Time is luck, and Phebe's luck ran out. We lost a dedicated, hard-working, loyal, loving, selfless teammate and K9 family member that blessed our lives for more than a decade.

After years of training together, Rumble and Phebe developed into a premier team that did our difficult and dangerous MET job with surgical precision. By the end of her watch, Rumble and Phebe had racked up 116 bite apprehensions of violent grow site suspects over a 10-year period. The number of suspects who surrendered before being subjected to Phebe's physical control is eight times that, at approximately 800. Of the more than 900 armed suspects the Fur Missile caught, approximately 85 percent of them were illegal nationals from Mexico, smuggled here by cartel-run DTO groups.

To put the significance of these numbers in perspective, we must remember that these men were not only cultivating marijuana illegally; they were also poisoning and destroying a diversity of wildlife species and waterways. And considering the record drought that ravaged California in recent years, the massive amount of water diverted and stolen by clandestine outdoor growers (approximately 1.3 billion gallons in 2013 and 2014 alone) was significant. Apprehending these suspects restored the natural balance of the waterways. Also, since most of the growers armed themselves to defend their crop from any threats, removing them from our wildlands benefitted the safety of both people and the ecology (outdoor enthusiasts, anglers, hunters, law enforcement teams, wildlife).

Along with her MET teammates, Phebe was the first K9 recognized for her exemplary career by the California legislature through resolution award ceremonies in January 2017 (see Addendum page 250). Members from both parties in the Assembly and Senate met the Fur Missile and our team members. This opportunity educated them about the magnitude of the DTO trespass grow problem as both a public safety threat and an environmental atrocity. It highlighted a career moment for us all.

I thought of that first deadly mission with Rumble and Phebe in June 2012, and how the Fur Missile saved us that day. She catalyzed a brotherhood among allied-agency operators that changed our history. Phebe both amplified and personified the passion and dedication of conservation officers nationwide. She is missed terribly. 🌿

K9 Phebe:
– Start of Watch: April 2008
– End of Watch: July 2018

N 37 05' 629"
W 121 52' 942"

CHAPTER 08

THE WILD WEST ABOVE SOQUEL CREEK: ENVIRONMENTAL DESTRUCTION IN THE SANTA CRUZ MOUNTAINS

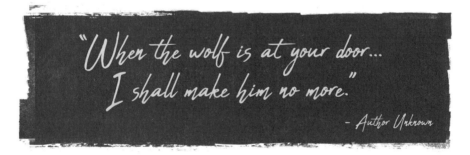

"When the wolf is at your door...
I shall make him no more."

– Author Unknown

JUNE 14, 2016 – HIGHLAND WAY – SANTA CRUZ MOUNTAINS

My cell phone rang as I rolled up the 101 into the Silicon Valley and headed to an allied-agency MET operation meeting. Excited to see Quinn's name on the screen, I answered right away. Even with my phone volume peaked, I could barely hear his whispers. Quinn ran a small scouting mission with Jerry and B.B. (Jerry's patrol boat supervisor and my friend since I trained him in cadet academy 11 years prior). His whispers alarmed me and indicated one of two things: either they were still deep in the woods and had confirmed an active grow site, or they had just seen and/or contacted suspects.

I pulled over onto the side of the freeway to better hear Quinn's SITREP. He

Reclaiming wilderness areas is tough work. Conservation officers often cut marijuana plants by hand before removal.

told me they did not see suspects, but he did confirm plants in one of possibly two plots halfway down the canyon. The trio was concealed in the brush just off a T-intersection along a well-established trail through the grow. Quinn's team would wait until the coast was clear to move up and out of the canyon.

The discovery excited Quinn and me. This environmentally sensitive area received a significant influx of cartel-run DTO trespass grow operations. The cartels operated undetected in this region for several years. Game on.

Highland Way — where Quinn found the grow — sat atop a steep redwood-forested ridge encompassing both large private tracts, as well as public outdoor enthusiast sections, including the Sierra Azul Midpeninsula Open Space Preserve. Sierra Azul, an 18,000-acre expanse of remote public land, spread into both Santa Cruz and Santa Clara counties. That made it popular for nature hikes, mountain biking and horseback riding. Other public recreation spots around Highland Way included Camp Loma (a children's outdoor skills development summer camp) and the Demonstration Forest (a premier mountain biking park). These properties sat above Soquel Creek, one of the last remaining Central Coast spawning channels for migrating steelhead.

We needed to plan and execute a MET operation on the complex as soon as possible. The Santa Clara County side of the preserve, above the city of Los Gatos, marked where a cartel ambush nearly shot my squad partner, Mojo, to death in 2005. Our allied-agency MET spent the next decade saturating the area to make sure DTO crews didn't reestablish operations. Cartel growers knew they faced aggressive apprehension efforts if they tried, including the use of K9 and deadly force engagements if necessary. To our satisfaction, we did not encounter any significant cartel-run grows in the Sierra Azul region since that horrible August day in 2005.

However, with a large, dense forest and plenty of water surrounding Highland Way just into Santa Cruz County, cartel DTO cells didn't need to move far to continue operations. With no Santa Cruz County law enforcement agencies willing to risk working DTO trespass grows, cartel cells jumped the county line to continue production without obstructions. We made this region of Santa Cruz County a priority.

JUNE 28, 2016 – HIGHLAND WAY – SANTA CRUZ MOUNTAINS

On the day of the mission, we conducted the ops briefing hours before first light. We gathered a full complement of allied-agency personnel and local district warden support. Military team leader/trauma medic Mark and his team of CANG operators, the district area Cal-Fire battalion chief, and wardens Bones and Jake rounded out the headcount. Without assistance from local law enforcement agencies, we held the bare minimum number of operators needed to pull off the operation safely. During our briefing, I reminded everyone of the day's officer safety concerns, following Quinn's logistics and contingency breakdown. Knowing the firepower and violent history of the cartel crews working the area, I reminded our team to keep their heads on a swivel and be ready, as events could get western, and fast.

After convoying to our drop point, we stacked up on the edge of Highland Way and conducted a final equipment and radio check before descending off the edge of the road. Sliding cross-country down the steep hillside, we hit the grow complex's T-intersection about 200 yards below the road. Quinn found his bearings and scanned the area with his carbine. A well-worn trail contained numerous man tracks going in both directions.

Quinn stood up and moved us down the trail, with Rumble and his new K9, Champ, not far behind. Champ recently graduated our K9 academy, and this marked his first large-scale MET operation.

Shang and Mak provided rifle support and K9 cover behind Rumble, with me behind them. Markos took up the tail gunner position. Jerry headed up our Quick Reaction Force in the point position, with Tango serving as the number two long gunner behind Jerry. A helicopter-operations expert, Tango would serve double-duty, running helicopter operations as well. Rich, Bones and Jake staged on Highland Way, ready to interdict any grower activity and assist us with suspect transport to jail.

That the trail was well-worn allowed us to remain quiet as we moved to the south. About 300 yards down the path, Quinn spotted movement ahead and stopped our team. We all took a knee as Rumble worked K9 Champ up to the front of our stack.

Within seconds, a single grower appeared 25 yards ahead, oblivious to our presence. He moved silently and was dressed in subdued camouflage clothing. With our team set up in a hasty ambush formation, we let him close the gap to us. Twenty yards. Fifteen yards. Ten yards. When the grower closed in on 10 feet away, we announced our presence quietly. The grower looked up, saw our point team fanned out and covering him with weapons, and looked around for

The MET entry and K9 apprehension team take a knee during the Highland Way operation.

an escape route. When he spotted Champ locked on him and ready to engage, he decided against it.

Shang handcuffed and detained the suspect on the edge of the trail. Quinn, Mak, Rumble and Champ covered the area ahead. With one suspect in custody and our team not even in the grow complex yet, we needed to hold the suspect there and avoid becoming compromised. I called two of our military teammates from the QRF to watch the grower, and Shang transferred custody to them before moving back into formation on our point team. Although pleased we caught this grower, I became concerned. Maintaining custody of the first catch of the day put two team members out of commission, stretching our already low numbers even thinner.

We resumed our stalk down the trail. Within 100 yards, we saw the start of

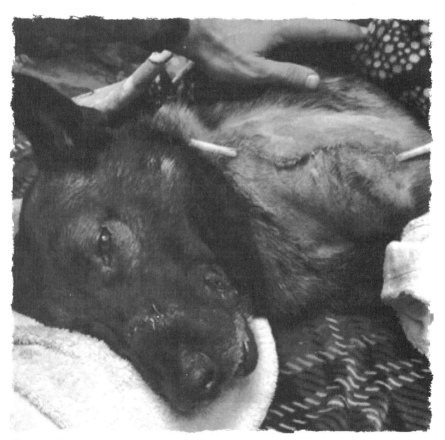

Some cartel growers develop counter-K9 tactics. This K9, just out of surgery, was stabbed during an apprehension operation.

the grow. Ahead of us, 4-foot-tall plants grew everywhere, with a huge camp and kitchen complex on the western edge of the plot. Camouflage tarps and a grove of redwoods made the camp invisible from the air.

We spotted three growers moving under the tarps through our binoculars. All three carried large, fixed-blade knives on their belts and what looked like handgun holsters. Oblivious to our presence, they focused on making breakfast before their workday. Unfortunately for them, that workday never came.

At a snail's pace, we closed the gap to the camp, using the marijuana plants and existing vegetation as concealment. After surrounding them on three sides just 20 yards away, we positioned Champ into a line of sight toward the camp. Some cartel DTO growers developed counter-K9 tactics by dedicating one person to take a dog bite while another tries to fatally stab the dog. However, we're quick learners, and we adjusted for this scenario.

Rumble announced our presence. As expected, all three men reached for their belts. Rumble released Champ and gave him the command to apprehend. Champ launched toward the lead grower but stopped halfway. The intensity of the operation, coupled with the high energy of our team, overwhelmed our new K9. Champ was just a week out of the K9 academy, and this was common behavior for new dual-purpose K9s during their first live missions. K9s must be conditioned through exposure to real-world operations before they perform under pressure. Champ needed time and experience.

Frustrated that his K9 didn't engage, Rumble sprinted toward the now fleeing growers, with Quinn, Shang and Mak running closely behind. Markos and I held back in the camp as the rest of our point team chased the three suspects downhill through a huge plot of tall marijuana plants. Our operators soon put handcuffs on two of the three runners. One of the men slipped away through the thick brush.

Rumble, Quinn and Mak escorted the two suspects back uphill to the camp complex, while I called our CANG operators from the QRF to bring our first suspect up. We converted the camp into a makeshift detention center for the three men.

With Shang and the CANG operators watching the suspects, Quinn gathered essential evidence throughout the camp. Tango and Jerry covered our backtrail. Rumble, K9 Champ, Markos and I stacked up to clear the next marijuana plot uphill from the camp to search for more growers in the first light of day.

Marijuana buds hang for drying in the Highland Way grow complex.

Champ alerted minutes later only 50 yards above the main camp. Concealed in marijuana plants, we focused on a small tent barely visible in the brush 30 yards ahead. Before I could pull up my binoculars, another grower popped into view near the tent. He walked downhill on the plot's main trail, heading right for us. Separated from the main camp and the rest of his crew, we knew this guy was the grow boss. He dressed all in black and carried a small, half-full garbage bag in his left hand. Clueless to our presence, he headed toward the main camp below.

At 15 yards, the boss saw us and stopped. Twirling the trash bag in his hand, he grinned and looked us over with a vacant look in his eyes. We couldn't tell if he was under the influence or just wired to fight, but his 1,000-yard stare alarmed me. We knew this look from cartel growers before, and it always meant a fight.

When we identified ourselves a second later, the grower maintained his grin, dropped the bag in his left hand and reached behind his back with his right hand. Rumble ordered Champ to apprehend, hoping his new K9 partner would engage this time. Still overwhelmed, Champ ran forward, but stopped a few feet ahead of us, again unsure of what to do. Without hesitation, Rumble sprinted ahead and tackled the grow boss before he could pull a weapon.

Rumble released control of the man and yelled to Markos and I, "You guys take him! I need to clear that tent!" Considering we now stood in a perfect field of fire, it was a good call.

The grow boss resisted our efforts to handcuff him with everything he had. Markos worked on his left hand as I worked on controlling his right. All the while, the suspect thrashed, kicked at our feet and swung punches while Markos tried to power his right hand behind his back. I noticed the grip of a handgun sticking out from the man's waistband behind his back. With his hand just inches away from the pistol, I worked on his right arm with all my strength, finally subduing him after several personal weapon strikes. The grow boss finally gave up. Markos handcuffed him while I secured and cleared his pistol, which we later learned was stolen from Washington state.

With the suspect secure, Markos looked up and said, "That was close, bud. Didn't see that pistol in his back. It was so well-hidden."

I nodded in agreement as my heart rate settled, feeling thankful the grow boss never got the extra second or two to use his pistol on us.

Rumble and Champ cleared the tent during the struggle. Fortunately, it was the grow boss' personal camp, and it was empty, with no evidence of others using it.

We escorted the man back to the main camp and transferred him to Shang and the rest of our security team. With the grow boss and his three minions secured, we stacked up again to clear the rest of the site. We discovered the growers diverted water from two tributaries of Soquel Creek to irrigate the 7,000-plant grow.

With our security team holding down the main complex, Rumble, K9 Champ, Markos, Tango, Jerry and I formed a hasty apprehension element and backtracked down the main trail. We continued north into uncharted territory. Although not quite as well-worn as the south trail, the path looked regularly used, with two recent sets of man tracks all over it.

A half-mile up the trail, we reached an intersection. The bisecting path descended downhill through a dense patch of brush into another redwood forest. As we moved through the brush wall, we spotted thousands of marijuana plants laid out in terraced rows covering half a football field below us. Rumble spotted a grower at the bottom of the steep incline. The grower froze in place and looked up in our direction before moving farther down the mountain and out of sight.

With Champ overwhelmed, we announced and identified ourselves. Rumble became our K9 and sprinted downhill, with Champ, Markos and me running closely behind. I'll never know how Rumble avoided tripping over one of the numerous plant holes, rocks or uneven dirt terraces during his sprint, but he made it down the hill in record time. The rest of us bounded left and right to avoid the minefield of trip hazards on our way down the mountain.

We came upon a dirt cliff that dropped 10 feet straight down to the camp and kitchen area. Laid out smooth and flat on a hand-excavated dirt floor, the camp complex spanned approximately 10 feet across and ended in a wall of thick brush and redwood trees. Unknown to us at the time, a second grower in the camp heard the chaos in the grow site above. He pushed his way through the camp's brush perimeter to get away, thinking we hadn't noticed.

Running full-speed, Rumble reached the dirt cliff at the bottom of the plot and jumped across it with everything he had, sailing over the camp and landing in the brush wall. He broke through the brush wall in an instant and spotted the second grower only 20 yards ahead. The grower, shocked by the sight of our relentless K9 handler flying through the air over his camp and landing right behind him, ran straight into a large redwood tree. The collision shattered his elbow and forearm, sending the grower to the ground. Holding his arm in agony, the grower rolled onto his back and looked up to the silhouette of Rumble standing above him against the morning sun.

Now on scene, I covered the team while Markos helped Rumble take the man into custody. After handcuffing the grower, Markos and Rumble treated his wounds before escorting him to the main trail. Tango and Jerry cleared and maintained security in the site. Unfortunately, the first grower we spotted was long gone.

It took all day to eradicate and remove a total of 10,000 budded marijuana plants from both grow sites, so we didn't have time to reclamate either complex during the mission. We would need to come back to remove all the camp and grow waste, irrigation piping, fertilizers and chemicals. In fill-and-flow fashion, we cut off the water flow through the poly pipe irrigation lines diverting water from the Soquel Creek tributaries into several large check dams within the complexes. Better than nothing.

We never found one of the three growers in the first camp, or the first grower we spotted in the northern grow complex. However, our team caught five of the seven men operating within both sites. We put in a good effort, especially considering our K9's rookie performance.

Typical of DTO trespass grows, the five cartel operatives we caught turned out to be Mexican nationals here illegally. A cartel smuggled them across our

Toxic Qu Furan poison, such as the kind inside this bottle found at the Highland Way grow complex, is banned in the United States.

MET operators hold market-ready, poisoned marijuana bud recovered from the Highland Way mission.

southern border for their horticultural skills. We booked all five suspects into the Santa Cruz County jail facility that afternoon for a mix of charges, including illegal marijuana cultivation, felony firearms possession and use, assault on a peace officer and several environmental crimes.

In the court proceedings, all but the grow boss pled guilty early in the process. Also typical for apprehended DTO suspects, the four that did plead guilty were released on low bail amounts and failed to show up at their sentencing hearings. However, an allied-agency team in northern California later caught one of the fugitives working in another DTO grow site.

The grow boss faced up to 10 years in prison for multiple crimes, including the most serious firearms charges. Given the steep penalty he faced, and against the advice of his attorney, the ringleader took the case to a jury trial and pleaded not guilty. Several months later, Quinn, Markos and I testified during the grow boss's preliminary hearing in Santa Cruz Superior Court. The boss seemed determined to test our case in open court the week of his jury trial, but he suddenly settled the case, pleading guilty to most of the charges before the jury-selection process. His sentencing didn't warrant celebration. What got another cartel grower a 5-year prison sentence in Santa Clara County (see Chapter 2) for the same felony assault on a peace officer just four years prior, yielded just 180 days of electronic monitoring for our defendant. Essentially free on six months of probation and mandated to wear an electronic monitoring bracelet during that time, the grow boss laughed at his sentence. He got a slap on the wrist despite being in the United States illegally, committing heinous public safety and environmental crimes, and fitting the federal criteria of a deportable felon.

Federal Immigration and Customs Enforcement (ICE) agents monitored this case closely, and the grow boss didn't laugh long. After walking out of the court building following his sentencing, a van full of agents pulled up, handcuffed him and took him into custody again. Over the next 72 hours, the grow boss was processed and deported back to Mexico, physically unable to do any more harm to our nation's wildlife resources.

At least for a while.

NOVEMBER 2016 - HIGHLAND WAY - SANTA CRUZ MOUNTAINS

With a nonstop operational season, we didn't make it back to the Highland Way site for reclamation until four months later. Some volunteers worked with us for the first time. They were comprised of licensed medicinal marijuana growers and legislators sympathetic to the environmentally conscious side of the cannabis industry. Like us, these folks wanted to see our wildlife, waterways and public lands protected from the devastation caused by DTO cultivation groups. We shared in the fight against a common enemy.

During the operation, we removed several tons of camp and kitchen infrastructure, dismantled the site's check dams and water impoundments and removed miles of black irrigation line. We hiked out together, tired and proud. Making history by bringing an unorthodox, but like-minded, environmentally conscious team of legislators, cannabis growers and spec ops law enforcement operators together to turn bad into good was rewarding. I felt satisfied knowing that this progressive operation would spread our message throughout the cannabis industry and well beyond. 🌿

N 37 05' 321"
W 121 51' 647"

CHAPTER 09

GUNFIGHT TWO ON SIERRA AZUL: DÉJÀ VU 11 YEARS LATER

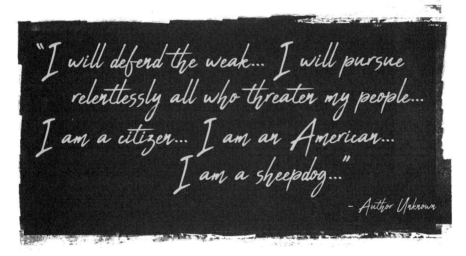

"I will defend the weak... I will pursue relentlessly all who threaten my people... I am a citizen... I am an American... I am a sheepdog..."

— Author Unknown

JUNE 30, 2017 – OPEN SPACE PRESERVE – SANTA CRUZ MOUNTAINS

Quinn and Jerry batted a thousand, finding at least one active marijuana growing operation in the Highland Way area of the Soquel Creek watershed each season since 2015. They'd scouted this remote area often, searching for cartel cells running marijuana grows unobstructed by the county sheriff's office.

When Quinn called me on that day, I had flashbacks to his excited whispers from the previous season. With their scout completed, and now far away from the grower trail, Quinn spoke in full volume to share the discovery. He and Jerry found another well-used trail and followed it to marijuana plants, a waterline and tent structures — all indicators of a DTO trespass complex.

The site stood a few miles from our 2015 and 2016 operations off of Highland Way, although the site was still located above and within the Soquel Creek watershed. Located between Loma Prieta Avenue and Highland Way, and adjacent to the Midpeninsula Open Space Preserve's SA32 gated Rattlesnake Gulch Road, this grow was in uncharted territory. The Sierra Azul Preserve — an 18,000-acre expanse of wilderness in Santa Cruz and Santa Clara counties — wrapped around the site. A well-prepared DTO cell had ambushed our allied-agency team on Aug. 5, 2005, within the Santa Clara County portion of Sierra Azul.

JULY 7, 2017 – SIERRA AZUL – SANTA CRUZ MOUNTAINS

Although we expected conflict, this felt different. The last time I took on a cartel-hunting op in Sierra Azul 11 years ago, my friend and partner almost died in my arms. That took place so long ago that none of today's team members had ever operated in this preserve before. But for me, the 11-year gap seemed like yesterday.

Quinn built the right team in less than a week. I reminded everyone of the violent history of the area and the aggressive DTO cells we encountered, including the gunfight in 2005. No one needed to hear it because we train and prepare with the expectation that every mission will turn deadly, but the extra reminder felt necessary.

We briefed in the darkness of the Santa Cruz Mountains. As with our last few ops near Highland Way, we arrived with a large enough team to handle anything we encountered, but not so large as to compromise our hunting and apprehension effectiveness. No matter how good the fieldcraft, a large team meant more noise.

Given the added officer and public safety danger of the mission, we added three K9 apprehension teams to the mix. Rumble paired up with K9 Champ, a completely changed dog this season following his mission failure the year prior on the Highland Way operation. Following that frustrating day, Rumble continued to train hard with K9 Champ outside of operations. Now honed into a decisive, confident apprehension and detection K9, we knew we were in good hands with Champ.

New to our MET, and assisting on the K9 team, came Buck and his dog, K9 Zoe. Buck was a motivated, energetic, hard-working game warden who always carried a positive attitude, and who also played a pretty mean guitar around the

Buck and K9 Zoe hold security with Quinn and Shang on a grower trail during the Sierra Azul operation.

campfire. Buck waited four years for a vacancy on our team, and he jumped on the opportunity when it did.

In 2016, Buck received his first K9, and 2-year-old Zoe joined our team. Like Phebe and Champ, Zoe was a slightly smaller Belgian Malenois, and one of the fastest, most agile K9s we've had the privilege of welcoming to our team. Now teammates, and each with a young, competent K9 at their sides, Rumble and Buck seemed unstoppable. By the end of 2016, they physically apprehended 37 armed growers. Another 63 gave up before contact with the dogs. They logged a staggering 100 apprehensions in only one season, a number unheard of up to that point. Not a shot was fired during those arrests. While bite apprehensions may sound brutal, a skilled apprehension K9 saves both operator and suspect lives.

Santa Clara County MET deputies Bark, K9 Nas and Fleck rounded out our K9 pack on the day's op. Along with Cole, they served as a blocking-force team that would come up from the south and hold on the perimeter of the grow while our primary entry team cleared the complex from the north.

From our MET, Tango would stay back and run the landing zone, coordinating eradication and reclamation operations later in the day with the California Highway Patrol (CHP) helicopter crew. Rich, our Cal-Fire ally, would assist Tango in the LZ. Given his knowledge of the area, Rich would also function as a critical incident coordinator if events turned bad.

With everyone squared away on our plan, we convoyed to the starting point of our hike on Loma Prieta Avenue. We moved through the gate onto Rattlesnake Gulch Road to keep our noise to a minimum. Riding shotgun with Quinn in his truck, we said little on our way down the rough dirt road.

At the drop-off point, we parked the vehicles and conducted a final equipment and comms check before stacking up. Jerry took point, given his familiarization with the site, and covered the trail ahead of us with his POF carbine. Rumble and K9 Champ followed Jerry, with Markos next in the stack providing K9 cover. I tracked behind them.

Quinn took up as point man of our QRF. He kept his team 25 yards behind our point unit. Buck and K9 Zoe followed next, with Shang providing carbine cover close behind our secondary K9 team. With a second K9 team in the QRF, we could split up and still apprehend suspects if the grow complex's trail system or terrain warranted. The triple-K9 threat granted us advantages to fill and flow around any issues we encountered.

We descended over the edge of Rattlesnake Gulch Road and navigated the near-vertical bank to the creek below. Steep, and covered in a thick layer of loose dirt and leaf litter, we mostly slid down the trail. Even in midsummer, the creek flowed strong, indicating the uphill tributaries flowed as well. With plenty of water, it became easy to see why the suspects picked the site.

Barely a stone's throw across the creek, we made out the grower trail in the dim, pre-sunrise light. The path ascended the steep bank over a narrow, hard-packed dirt spine that disappeared in the trees above us. Utilizing the hard-packed dirt in a shadowy area, the growers did an admirable job of concealing their trail.

For the next hour, we followed the grow trail another 200 yards, gaining elevation with each step. None of us liked assaulting a grow from below, but sometimes the terrain and grow-access points afforded no other option. Without our preferred uphill tactical advantage, I became painfully aware of our vulnerability from above during the stalk. This looked too much like the climb during the 2005 Sierra Azul mission, when we were ambushed. I felt on edge. I radioed everyone to keep their eyes peeled and reminded Jerry up front to scan ahead and be ready to engage with his carbine.

Jerry spotted the first sign of the grow: a tent or tarp structure concealed in a dense cluster of redwood trees 50 yards above us. After watching it for five minutes and picking it apart with our optics, we noticed no movement and continued our climb.

Twenty-five yards farther, we ran into a well-worn bisecting trail leading southwest. Given its location, we concluded it must run along the bottom perimeter of the grow site. It likely led to our blocking-force K9 team's location to the south. Given the trail's significance, we needed to lock it down. Suspects could slip out of our apprehension net or sneak in behind us as we climbed.

I separated our entry element at the intersection, putting the QRF K9 team on the bisecting trail to ambush any suspects using it. In seconds, Quinn, Buck, K9 Zoe and Shang concealed themselves along the trail's edge.

With the QRF settled in place, I cleared Jerry to move us up the main trail. Our point team turned into a small, four-man K9 apprehension element. The early morning stillness sounded unusually quiet. We heard none of the typical early morning wildlife sounds. No birds chirping or flying around. No mammals moving through the vegetation. Nothing. It once again reminded me of the dead calm right before the 2005 ambush. I scanned over my pistol sights, hearing only my heartbeat in the silence.

That silence changed when a strong wind kicked up. The intense sound of the

Marijuana Enforcement Team game wardens from the California Department of Fish and Wildlife, including K9 Champ, hold the area around the grower's kitchen during the Sierra Azul operation.

wind blowing through massive redwood branches sounded surreal. We didn't hesitate to take advantage of the wind's sound-covering effects, and we glided smoothly toward the structure Jerry spotted.

The empty structure turned out to be a recently used grower kitchen. The kitchen stocked fresh food, a propane stove, and other kitchen and hygiene supplies. A camouflage tarp and the dark canopy of redwoods hid the kitchen. Some of the growers' dinner still rested in a pot on the stove from the night before, indicating they had not made it down for breakfast yet. The growers created a makeshift bathing area in the middle of a narrow Soquel Creek tributary. A black poly pipe with a cut-off valve supplied water. Between the bathing area and kitchen, the trail continued up the mountain at an even steeper angle.

Realizing the growers would soon arrive for breakfast, we set up an ambush around the kitchen and waited. From my position deep in the shadows of the kitchen, I could see Rumble, K9 Champ and Markos just outside the structure, covering the trail above. Slightly out of view and concealed in the bathing area, Jerry covered the short distance to Rumble and Markos with his long rifle.

Fifteen minutes passed with no movement from above. The wind finally died down, so we could hear anything moving around us. After 40 minutes of silence, and pushing late into the morning, I called it. We got up and climbed up the steep trail with our weapons at the high ready.

The gunman's movement appeared as a blur out of the thousands of marijuana plants above on the steep trail. He swung a big, chrome revolver in his right hand toward us after spotting Rumble and Champ. In a rush to get off the X, Rumble dove to the right as he announced the threat and dropped Champ's leash. With confidence, Champ launched uphill and bit the grower in the shoulder, pushing the pistol off target. Rumble drew his pistol and engaged the gunman with a rapid volley of shots.

As Rumble engaged and moved laterally, Jerry moved with him, covering above for additional threats. Markos and I moved to the right with Rumble, shifting our field of fire up toward the gunman to support our partner and avoid a blue-on-blue crossfire disaster.

The gunman went down and out of view somewhere in a thick brush patch above the kitchen area. We held in a tight perimeter, concealed along the edge of the main trail just above the kitchen. After a quick check on our K9 handler, and finding him unscathed, I called a SITREP. Thankfully, none of us took fire before Rumble engaged the suspect. Like the Sierra Azul gunfight more than a

Pictured is one of two loaded pistols found on a cartel suspect in the Sierra Azul DTO grow complex. Every raid on a grow site brings with it the risk of a gunfight. K9s can offset that risk by eliminating threats before a shot is fired. The growers still manage to kill K9s years later when the dogs develop cancer. The growers' poisonous Carbofuran is a likely culprit.

decade earlier, this engagement lasted only seconds. However, we were not out of the woods yet. We knew more gunmen waited in the complex ahead of us.

I moved our QRF up to widen our perimeter and check on the condition of the gunman. Meanwhile, Jerry, Rumble and Champ held and covered the uphill trail. I radioed Tango to function as our information relay from the landing zone with his powerful patrol truck radio. Tango made essential notifications to our dispatch center, while Quinn, Shang, Buck and K9 Zoe moved to us. With our QRF in place, I instructed Quinn and Markos to check on the downed suspect, while Shang set up a helicopter landing zone. Regardless of the gunman's condition, we needed helicopter support to remove him from the site for any trauma care.

I put Buck and K9 Zoe on the uphill side of the trail on the lower edge of the grow site near Rumble and K9 Champ. They covered the top of the perimeter and

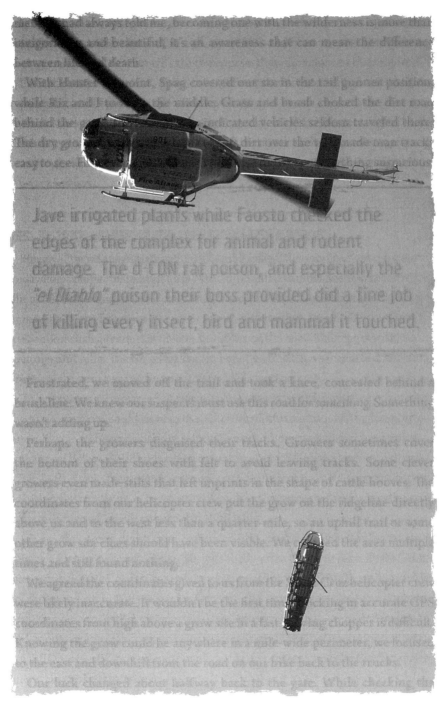

...had always told me, becoming one with the wilderness is more than [...] and beautiful, it's an awareness that can mean the difference between life and death.

With [...], Spag covered our six in the tail gunner position while [...] and I took the middle. Grass and brush choked the dirt road behind the [...] vehicles seldom traveled there. The dry ground was [...] to uncover the [...] made man-tracks easy to see. [...] suspicious.

Jave irrigated plants while Fausto checked the edges of the complex for animal and rodent damage. The d-CON rat poison, and especially the "el Diablo" poison their boss provided did a fine job of killing every insect, bird and mammal it touched.

Frustrated, we moved off the trail and took a knee, concealed behind [...] brushline. We knew our suspects must use this road for something. Something wasn't adding up.

Perhaps the growers disguised their tracks. Growers sometimes cover the bottom of their shoes with felt to avoid leaving tracks. Some clever growers even made suits that left imprints in the shape of cattle hooves. The coordinates from our helicopter crew put the grow on the ridgeline directly above us and to the west less than a quarter-mile, so an uphill trail or some other grow site clues should have been visible. We [...] the area multiple times and still found nothing.

We agreed the coordinates given to us from the [...] helicopter crew were likely inaccurate. It wouldn't be the first time. Picking an accurate GPS coordinates from high above a grow site in a fast-moving chopper is difficult. Knowing the grow could be anywhere in a mile-wide perimeter, we focused to the east and downhill from the road on our hike back to the trucks.

Our luck changed about halfway back to the gate. While checking the [...]

A Cal-Fire Huey flies inbound to extract an injured cartel suspect following an officer-involved shooting incident in the Sierra Azul DTO grow complex.

GUNFIGHT TWO ON SIERRA AZUL: DÉJÀ VU 11 YEARS LATER

supported Rumble as needed. In addition to being a K9 handler, Buck served as our warden association president and a direct pipeline for support following an officer-involved shooting. His knowledge helped Rumble immensely throughout the day. In the event that media crews reported the wrong information, which happened during the 2005 Sierra Azul OIS incident, and at Rumble's request, I called to inform his family that he and the rest of the team were safe.

Markos and Quinn searched for the suspect in the brush and found him in a small drainage above the kitchen. They found the incoherent grower doubled over and injured from two bullet wounds. Both operators provided trauma care immediately. They stabilized the gunman until he could be moved to a hospital for further treatment. Over the hill in Santa Clara County, Cal-Fire's helicopter crew spooled up its bird from the Alma station, approximately 45 minutes away.

Besides the gunman's revolver, the fanny pack around his waist contained a

MET operators and a Cal-Fire medic move an injured cartel suspect to the landing zone for evacuation after the Sierra Azul OIS incident.

high-capacity automatic pistol. It again reminded us of the aggressive mindset of the DTO crews working this region.

With Buck, Rumble and their K9s covering, Shang searched for an ideal helicopter landing zone in the middle of the massive marijuana grow. The huge site hosted 11,000 mature plants spread out over the entire ridgeline. With dense redwood forest on top of the ridge less than 100 yards above the plot, Shang could see why the growers chose this area. He suspected the main camp must be somewhere in the tree line above, giving the growers an ideal tactical advantage when patrolling their grow site below.

Shang pulled off his backpack and placed an orange reflective vest on the ground. Used to mark the center of the landing zone, helicopter crews can easily spot this high-visibility beacon. With no large tree branches above Shang's chosen spot, this LZ looked safe for the incoming helicopter's hoist cable, rescue basket and medic insertion.

I called my captain when safe to do so after the gunfight. Unable to reach him, I called Nate. Unfortunately for our MET, Nate no longer served as my direct boss. He had been promoted to the two-star assistant chief position to run statewide operations. Although great for the agency, Nate's promotion left a critical vacancy in our spec ops chain of command. I missed working with him on MET business.

Nate, off duty, worked from home that day, but as always he answered his cell phone when he saw I was calling. I gave him a quick rundown of our status, and he was relieved to hear our team was safe. Nate and I talked throughout the day to ensure he was getting real-time, accurate information as the operation progressed.

After more phone calls with other members of my command staff and allied-agency law enforcement supervisors from Santa Cruz County, we learned that we would be on our own to clear the rest of the grow, eradicate it and maintain security of the entire site. The California Department of Justice (DOJ) forensic team out of the Sacramento office would cover CSI and OIS tasks instead of local agencies. However, the team wouldn't arrive on scene until the following morning.

Less than 30 minutes after Shang set up the LZ, we heard the thump of the big Huey's blades chopping the air above us as it approached from the north. Shang vectored the helicopter in to our location. Within minutes, the Huey hovered 100 feet above us and a medic and a rescue basket descended on a hoist cable.

I briefed the medic as soon as he touched down. We secured the grower in the basket, and within seconds, the medic and suspect were off the ground on the hoist cable toward the hovering helicopter. It was déjà vu as I watched the medic and rescue basket get smaller and smaller, soon disappearing in the distance. This same Cal-Fire Huey rescued Mojo on that pivotal August day in 2005. Thankfully, one of the bad guys laid in the basket this time. I said a quick prayer of thanks and felt a wave of gratitude and pride, reflecting on how far we'd come since that challenging mission almost 12 years earlier.

Back at the site, we tightened our perimeter, bringing Cole, Bark, K9 Nas and Fleck to us. We needed to get the whole team back together before mapping out our next move.

Unfortunately, because of the officer-involved shooting, Rumble, Markos, Jerry and I needed to leave our teammates behind to answer a battery of questions about the incident. We regretted our departure, but we had no choice. Before the four of us left the grow, I split the team, holding a security element around the OIS site to preserve evidence until relief officers arrived. The second team would stalk out the rest of the complex's elaborate trail system and clear the remainder of the site before beginning the eradication phase of the operation. I put Shang in charge of operations in my absence, allowing Quinn to continue collecting the evidence he needed for the public safety and environmental crime case. With deep regret, the four of us started our hike back down to the Rattlesnake Gulch Road drop point.

Back at the helicopter LZ, Tango chomped at the bit to get up on the hill and help his brothers. With no other air assets needed then, he left the LZ and headed our way. Tango motored down the steep, rocky fire road, driving his truck all the way down to the growers' creek crossing trail we used earlier. Seeing Tango's truck parked at the creek as we descended was a relief. We climbed into his patrol vehicle, and he transported us back to the IC for debriefing. After dropping us off, Tango returned to the grow site to assist the rest of the team.

Shang's entry team cleared the 11,000-plant plot piece by piece, stalking toward the redwood forest at the top of the ridge. The team spotted a shadowed grove of redwoods that could provide an ideal spot for a DTO camp. The team held and assessed. While clearing the grove, the team discovered camouflaged tents hidden in the shadows. The tents held a pistol-gripped AK-47, an SKS with a 30-round magazine full of ammunition and a pistol-gripped pump-action, 12-gauge shotgun loaded with buckshot. Also of concern was a piece of deer bone. Growers had sharpened and coated the bone with poison to stab and kill our K9s. Clearly, this group of growers knew about our operations. Behind the

These poisoned marijuana buds found in the Sierra Azul DTO grow complex look ready for sale.

tents rested the growers' escape trail. It dropped steeply into a drainage behind the redwood forest.

The team realized that the camp's position in the trees at the top of the ridge made it almost impossible to approach undetected. Operators couldn't avoid walking into the gunmen's field of fire when moving through the grow site and would never see the hidden camp deep in the shadows until it was too late. During an early morning mission, operators would approach the encampment while looking straight into the rising sun. An inexperienced team could follow the main grow trail into this fatal funnel of high-caliber gunfire, incurring numerous casualties. This tactically sound, high-ground ambush site used the same layout as the gunmen we encountered on the other side of Sierra Azul in 2005. This crew belonged to the same violent DTO cell that engaged and almost killed my partner. Fortunately, the other gunmen from the camp were gone.

Their fresh tracks illustrated a rapid exit into the abyss of the dense Sierra Azul redwood forest to the east.

After clearing, searching and documenting the weapons and other evidence in the camp, Shang's entry team eradicated the grow site. Now mid-day, with temperatures in the triple digits, our small eradication team waited for support officers to arrive. They eradicated the massive plot of mature plants late into the evening.

Before my OIS interview at the DA's office, I took a conference call with Nate and Dave regarding the mission's chain of events. After hearing the mission breakdown, Nate and Dave sounded supportive and relieved that our MET ran the operation. The day's events illustrated the benefits of our team's tactics, operational protocol and training level.

The grow complex security-relief team arrived on scene well after sunset — a few hours after our entry team finished eradicating the entire area. The overnight team consisted of a complement of patrol wardens from across the state. They would secure the grow overnight until the DOJ forensic team arrived the following morning. Realizing that the gunmen who escaped could come back after dark and check on their losses, Shang and Tango mapped out a tactical plan and security positions for the inbound team. The relief team needed all the tactical advantages possible for its overnight stay. By midnight, all of our team members collapsed in hotel rooms, exhausted after a nonstop, 22-hour operation.

THREE DAYS LATER – YAAK VALLEY – MONTANA/ALBERTA BORDER

Out of California, and winded as I climbed the last 1,000 feet to my hidden meadow, my cell phone's vibration surprised me. I needed a break from operations to decompress, and I found myself disappointed to have coverage in this remote area. I answered when I saw it was my captain. The frustration in her voice was evident.

She needed to pass on orders that came from the top. Effective immediately, none of our team members could share suspect information with, or work with, federal ICE agents on any cartel-run DTO trespass grow-related operations. In October 2017, California passed its California Values Act, which prohibits state and local law enforcement from notifying ICE of possible illegal aliens, unless the suspects detained committed certain serious crimes within the past 15 years, among other things. Many

Fleeing cartel members left behind this tactical shotgun and other weapons, including a poisoned deer bone designed for stabbing K9s.

believed this new state law turned California into a "sanctuary state" for illegal aliens.

I was shocked. On top of the nature of the cartel's dangerous and environmentally destructive criminals, our policy obligated us to assist any federal agency when asked to do so. Additionally, the U.S. Fish and Wildlife Service's Code of Federal Regulations (CFR) deputized state game wardens as federal agents. In effect, this directive prevented us from working with an allied federal agency on the DTO trespass cultivation front. It could only negatively affect our mission: keeping violent and environmentally destructive criminals from threatening public safety and decimating our nation's wildlife, waterways and wildlands.

The United States, a country of immigrants, is blessed to be truly the land of the free, but these growers were not harmless people trying to provide for their families and chase the American dream. The architects of the sanctuary state doctrine failed to see how their policy protected thousands of cartel DTO operatives.

MET operator Buck is seen here with K9 Zoe, fresh out of the K9 academy.

The vast majority of the DTO trespass grow suspects we apprehended came into the country illegally, and the injured gunman on Sierra Azul was no exception. Smuggled across the border by his DTO to grow black-market marijuana, and having an extensive criminal history, he met the deportable felon criteria under U.S. federal immigration standards. Cut off from ICE enforcement assistance, the state court system in California processed his charges. As in the case of the grow boss we arrested near Highland Way in 2016, this grower could get off with a slap on the wrist in state court for multiple public safety and environmental charges, if he even showed up in court at all. Regardless of the penalty, he would remain in the country illegally, unimpeded to resume destructive and dangerous marijuana growing operations within our nation's wildlands.

Sharing in her frustration, I ended the call with my captain. I continued my ascent of the remote mountain, hopeful that other states did not make the same mistake as California and provide sanctuary for cartel felons.

To no one's surprise, the gunman from the Sierra Azul operation stopped showing up at court after his first appearance. There stood no chance to apprehend him during his first court appearance with ICE out of the picture. As of this writing more than a year later, the grower remains at large. Experience told me he is likely doing what all cartel growers do when they are not in custody or forced out of the country: growing more poisoned marijuana and destroying our nation's natural resources in another area.

Unfortunately for Buck and the rest of our team, the Sierra Azul mission went down as one of K9 Zoe's final MET operations. After only one complete and amazing MET season under her belt, Zoe was diagnosed with incurable cancer. She passed away in May 2018 at only two years old. Like K9 Phebe and my companion dog, Jordan, who is also dying of cancer, our team suspected their exposure to Carbofuran during grow operations may have caused the disease. Although K9 Zoe only worked with us for a single year, we felt lucky to work with her. Zoe's DTO suspect apprehensions kept us safe and prevented numerous gunfights. ✹

K9 Zoe:
– Start of Watch: Feb 16, 2017
– End of Watch: May 14, 2018

N 36 31' 039"
W 118 07' 508"

CHAPTER 10

CANNABIS REGULATION: ENFORCEMENT CHALLENGES BEYOND LEGALIZATION

> *"The earth provides enough to satisfy everyone's need, but not everyone's greed."*
>
> — Mahatma Gandhi

Tallying up the numbers from the start of the pilot program in July 2013 through December 2018, the MET's production level painted an ugly picture. During our first five years of operations, the unit completed 800 arrest, eradication and reclamation missions. On those missions, we destroyed 3 million poisoned marijuana plants, seized and destroyed 58,677 pounds (29 tons) of processed marijuana, made 973 felony arrests, seized 601 firearms, removed 899,945 pounds (450 tons) of grow site waste and other pollutants, recovered and removed 2.35 million feet (445 miles) of black poly pipe, removed 91,728 pounds (46 tons) of fertilizers, extracted 756 gallons of illegal toxic chemicals and dismantled 793 water-stealing dams and diversions from DTO grow complexes. Those dams stole approximately 12 billion gallons of water, mostly during the peak of California's drought period, costing California taxpayers. They would have taken another 12 billion gallons of much-needed drinking and agricultural irrigation water had we not eliminated the operations.

Although these numbers represented the high level of environmental damage done by DTOs to our wildlands, waterways and wildlife, they make up just a fraction of the total impact throughout the country. Keep in mind, the figures came from just the missions CDFW's MET participated in. Also, although we grew better over the last decade at finding, eliminating and restoring DTO grow sites, we found only a small percentage of the total number of cartel-run trespass grows throughout California, to say nothing of the rest of the country.

With cannabis legalization becoming more widespread throughout the country, including in California, I've lost count of how many people have asked me, "Now that pot's legal, you guys are out of a job, right?" People also frequently say, "We should just legalize weed so you guys can go do real game warden work." I wish it was that simple.

The misnomer that legalizing cannabis would alleviate both the domestic and cartel-run black markets — and their associated public safety and environmental crimes — did not prove out. As the 10 states that have legalized recreational marijuana cultivation (and the additional 23 that sanction medicinal marijuana distribution and use) discovered, cannabis regulation did not eradicate the dark side of the issue.

California, for example, legally sanctioned medical marijuana cultivation and distribution for more than two decades, starting with the passing of Proposition 215 in 1996. In 2016, the Golden State became the seventh state in the union to allow and regulate the cultivation and use of recreational cannabis. California is one of only six true Mediterranean climates in the world, and the best state in the country to grow cannabis almost year-round, making it the nation's epicenter for weed. As a result, the lucrative black market for California bud has never been higher.

Proponents of recreational and medicinal marijuana legalization argue that the market for DTO trespass marijuana would be eliminated if licensed cannabis is readily available. But with more than 85 percent of DTO trespass marijuana produced in California sold on the black market to Midwest and Eastern Seaboard states that do not allow recreational or medicinal cannabis use, legalization in California in its current form won't stop DTOs from using the Golden State's resources to fill nationwide demand for their product.

Proposition 64 (the Marijuana Legalization Initiative) reduced public

MET operators and CDFW biologists pause during a DTO trespass grow complex reclamation operation at 9,000 feet above Lone Pine in the eastern Sierra Nevada Mountains. Cartel-smuggled, banned poisons killed sensitive, high-altitude mammals at this site, including black bears and the endangered Sierra Nevada bighorn sheep.

and private land trespass marijuana-cultivation penalties from felonies to misdemeanors. This devastated efforts to protect our wildlife, wildlands and waterways. For juvenile trespass cultivation offenders, Prop. 64 reduced the penalty to an infraction, making the crime equal in severity to driving without a seatbelt in California. This shocked all of us in law enforcement, especially given the extensive outreach and education work we did to prevent this before the legislation passed.

Since our start in 2013, our MET conducted numerous presentations to a variety of constituent groups about the positive and negative effects of new cannabis legislation. Given our mutual love for wildlife and the outdoors, we wanted to ensure that new cannabis regulations deterred the public safety and environmental crimes engendered by outdoor trespass grow operations.

Using stories from our MET missions, we showed the magnitude of infiltration by cartel cells, the public safety threats and the damage done to wildlands. Whether we're showing students the dark side of the cannabis issue, or conveying our story to influential conservation, wildlife, animal rights and legislative groups, everyone attending these presentations was outraged. No matter where one stands on the issue — user or non-user, pro-cannabis or against — everyone was disgusted and emotionally moved when seeing the cartel's firepower, their anti-personnel and animal-killing booby traps, their trash-infested and polluted grow complexes and waterways, and the poisoned wildlife common to illegal marijuana grows.

Even after telling this story to thousands of people, the laws to further deter DTO trespass operations did not materialize in California. Instead, we experienced a reduction in DTO trespass grow deterrence. With these crimes watered down to a misdemeanor or infraction, a majority of sheriff's office marijuana-enforcement units stopped working DTO trespass grow cases entirely. Likewise, many DA offices in California refused to prosecute trespass grow cases. We knew after Prop. 64 passed in November 2016 we would mostly be on our own.

In fill-and-flow fashion, our MET developed a strategy to put the felony bite back into the criminal penalties associated with outdoor trespass grow operations. Illegally diverting streams and polluting waterways during cultivation operations were now felonies, so we used those jury-friendly charges to get cases filed and prosecuted throughout California. Using water illegally and spreading EPA-banned poisons like Carbofuran and its derivatives during

A marijuana plant, poisoned with the EPA-banned Furadan, grows at a cartel site in Sonoma County, California. Marijuana legalization in California failed to curb these grows.

MET officers clear a Furadan-poisoned DTO grow complex in Sonoma County, California, during filming for the NRA Patriot Profiles: Life of Duty *documentary series.*

trespass grow operations were also felonies, which also plays well with DAs. Almost every DTO-run grow site we encountered used these poisons.

Regardless of where juries stand on the cannabis issue, they always sympathized with the multitude of environmental crimes we stopped. No one likes to see the poisoning of sensitive waterways or the senseless killing of wildlife. When we added the firearms use and assault charges (felonies with significant penalties) against armed DTO suspects, DAs gained even more ammunition to prosecute and convict. Bottom line, if the cannabis issue could be removed from the equation, we could convict in even the most cannabis-sympathetic jurisdictions.

One of the most passionate and responsive organizations I've presented to on several occasions is a group of environmentally concerned cannabis growers in California. In 2015, I became the first law enforcement officer to speak at a series of pre-licensing California Growers Association (CGA) meetings. The unorthodox pairing of a statewide marijuana-enforcement tactical team leader working with and presenting to hundreds of formerly law-breaking cannabis farmers proved both interesting and exciting.

> With cannabis legalization becoming more widespread throughout the country, including in California, I've lost count of how many people have asked me, "Now that pot's legal, you guys are out of a job, right?" I wish it was that simple.

For years, these cannabis farmers operated in the black market behind the curtain of Proposition 215, avoiding law enforcement interaction as much as possible. With prohibition on its way out, these people made history by jumping out of their comfort zones and attending the meeting. Their responses during the presentation were overwhelming. I showed pictures of heavily armed cartel growers with blurred faces, punji pit booby traps and the poisoned carcasses of mountain lions, black bears, gray foxes, golden eagles, mule deer and other animals. These images prompted shouts of disgust and outrage. Some viewers looked away in sadness, and some even shed tears. That so few of the legal growers at the presentation were familiar with cartel-run DTO trespass grows surprised me.

About 30 commercial growers followed me to my truck after the presentation. They asked numerous questions, including the right steps to take during the licensing process and how to contact MET and my colleagues from our Watershed Enforcement Team (WET), which focuses on private-land cultivation-compliance issues. They gave me business cards and asked how they could help my team restore and reclaim cartel grow sites. They volunteered their time, money and personnel to jump in with us during our reclamation efforts. DTO trespass growers gave these legitimate growers a bad name.

We'd never had positive contact with growers before. What would have traditionally been a greeting with handcuffs became a meeting with handshakes. Over the last two seasons, we continued to work with legal grower groups, presenting at more of their functions. The percentage of growers who want to do things legally and be part of a unified front to stop the DTO's infiltration of our wildlands continued to grow. In fact, a handful of growers and cannabis industry attorneys put not only their time, but also their money, toward the cause by donating funds and developing a nonprofit foundation to spread awareness and aid in our mission.

As for the cannabis black market itself, it has yet to disappear. Granted, it's only been a year since the law change, but the results so far have not been favorable. Given the relatively high overhead and operating costs of cannabis dispensaries, and the unprecedented disclosure of taxable income generated from recreational and medicinal cannabis sales, the price of legal weed increased substantially. Since legalization, a lucrative incarnation of the black market developed. Black market cannabis remained cheaper to produce because growers never paid income taxes on their sales or property taxes on the land where the crop was produced. In fact, in many cases, they didn't even own the land, and instead illegally grew cannabis on public property. This development created a surge of growers and distributors who undercut legitimate cannabis farmers and distributors all over the country. This disparity in cannabis pricing placed a demand for the cheaper product, and unregulated and illegal cannabis sales continued to grow.

Even before our new cannabis laws took effect, farmers told me that regulation wouldn't make a difference to most growers. Business-savvy individuals explained the 80/20 rule to us early on. They said that of the total number of cannabis growers in California, only 20 percent or less would register for licensing and do business legally. The other 80 percent of growers preferred to fly under the radar, keeping their farms hidden from agency inspection and continuing to take their chances making tax-free, black-market profits, just as they've done for decades.

After analyzing the cannabis-license applications in 2017, the 80/20 rule proved true. For instance, in Humboldt County (one of California's largest cannabis-cultivation counties within the aptly named Emerald Triangle), approximately 2,300 growers applied for licensing following the implementation of new regulations. With a conservative estimate of 12,000 private-land cannabis cultivators operating within Humboldt County, fewer than 20 percent are licensed. This pattern held true for the rest of the state as well.

However, licensed farmers fought back by turning in black market growers to agencies like ours. Rightfully so, legal growers believed that if they must go through the high financial cost and exposure associated with licensing, so should everyone else.

Pictured is the result of the first allied-agency Santa Clara County Sheriff's Office MET grow complex reclamation in 2006. The event took place in the Mount Hamilton backcountry of Silicon Valley. Boy Scouts and Sheriff's Cadet Explorers assisted with the restoration. Press coverage of the event exposed the environmental damages of cartel-run trespass grow operations and the value of reclamation operations throughout the West Coast.

Although our MET's mission focused on illegal, cartel-run DTO trespass grow operations, game warden teams also focused on environmental and other crimes committed by the 80 percent of unlicensed private land growers throughout the state.

Our Watershed Enforcement Team (WET) and Marijuana Permitting Team (MPT), funded and developed from 2014 to 2017, has expanded ever since. These units discovered numerous environmental and public safety crimes during site inspections and/or search warrant details. It's no wonder some growers hold no desire to apply for a license and play by the rules. Given the multitude of crimes they committed, they have too much to lose.

Regardless of where juries stand on the cannabis issue, they always sympathized with the multitude of environmental crimes we stopped. No one likes to see the poisoning of sensitive waterways or the senseless killing of wildlife.

Concerned only with their bottom line, these growers couldn't care less about water quality, wildlife habitat — and in extreme cases — human life. Like outdoor DTO trespass grow sites, the worst private land cultivators steal and pollute water. They denude entire mountainsides of trees and other wildlife-supporting vegetation and pose human health hazards throughout their sites.

Other issues with cannabis legalization, especially concerning private land medicinal cannabis production, were the associated politics and loophole abuses by licensed growers. In pro-cannabis counties especially, enforcement teams like our WET and MPT units have been blocked from doing compliance checks on growers known to commit multiple environmental and health and safety crimes. Regardless of these crimes, they instructed our teams not to do inspections or serve search warrants. Instead, they gave growers a grace period through the licensing process. If the team is allowed to inspect them, we are only told to document environmental crimes and not eradicate any illegal plants. Thus, the incentives for grower compliance became minimal.

A helicopter removes poisoned marijuana site waste from the high-elevation Lone Pine grow complex in the eastern Sierra Nevada. Operations such as this one will continue despite marijuana legalization in California. The heavy cost of doing business legally pushes growers into illegal activity to keep prices down.

MET operators Doc and Shang utilize mules and horses during a reclamation mission in a wilderness area DTO trespass grow site. Stock animals are invaluable teammates where motorized vehicles and other support equipment are not allowed.

A MET K9 sits next to hundreds of pounds of processed black-market marijuana. Slated for nationwide distribution, this tainted product was interdicted immediately after being transferred into cartel vehicles from the grow site.

If we can't destroy high-dollar plants grown while numerous environmental violations are committed, we can't deter growers from committing such destructive crimes.

Even cartel-run DTOs played these politics and capitalized on our licensing grace period. As of this writing toward the end of the 2018 grow season, we witnessed a significant reduction in the number of remote DTO trespass grows on public lands. Although that appeared to be a positive outcome of cannabis legalization, there's a catch. The DTOs have cleverly shifted their focus to running grow operations on private properties. Knowing these properties will see little law enforcement pressure after landowners applied for a cannabis-

A MET K9 is pictured here with DTO trespass grow complex waste, waterline and infrastructure. A helicopter will later remove this. The MET works year-round on all phases (apprehension, eradication and reclamation) of our mission, even in the winter.

cultivation license, cartel cells produced their clandestine crop in California with impunity.

In a 2018 case, our MET combined forces with the U.S. Forest Service and the Sacramento area's California Multi-Jurisdictional Methamphetamine Enforcement Team (Cal-MMET) to raid multiple outdoor and greenhouse grows on two properties in the Central Valley. Both properties enrolled in the cannabis-licensing process. During the operation, we apprehended 17 DTO growers, seized several firearms and documented and charged the growers with numerous environmental crimes, including water pollution and illegal streambed alteration.

Prior to cannabis legalization, these DTO operatives would have been embedded in our wildlands. They no longer needed to operate grows in remote areas, at least if the licensing-process grace period was in effect. DTOs worked smarter — not harder — by focusing on low-lying agricultural lands that have easy access. The water they pollute now is used for legitimate crop irrigation and drinking water, making the damages just as severe as poisoning a pristine headwater in the mountains. So, although Proposition 64 reduced the number of remote public land trespass grows by at least 50 percent in 2018, it came at a significant cost. The environmental crimes these groups committed, and the public safety threat they generated, transplanted to locations closer to population centers instead of becoming eliminated.

Without a doubt, revenue turned out to be the biggest upside of cannabis legalization and regulation. Cannabis-licensing fees, for example, generated millions of dollars in revenue for regulatory agencies. For CDFW's MET, WET and MPT units, this meant much-needed funds for additional teams and personnel, compensation for the high number of overtime hours we worked, money for specialized tactical equipment to do our jobs safely and capital for helicopter and reclamation teams to clean up and restore DTO grow sites.

Still significantly understaffed, we were only able to reclaim 44 percent of the DTO trespass grow complexes we raided each season. Our agency and our outdoor-loving constituents would love to see that number much higher, with each site reclamated the day of our takedown mission or shortly thereafter. The funding generated from legalized cannabis can help us attain these goals.

With millions of cannabis users throughout the country, the demand for both black market and sanctioned cannabis production isn't slowing down as its use becomes more mainstream and accepted. Whether you are for or against cannabis legalization, and whether you're a user or non-user of cannabis products, we can all agree on one thing: the effects of legalized cannabis production should never encourage egregious environmental crimes and public safety threats. We must consider this when choosing to regulate cannabis and try to learn from the policy shortfalls in the states that have legalized it. With our agency's mandate to enforce compliance of legal cannabis-production facilities, coupled with the fight against public safety and environmental threats posed by DTO trespass cultivation operations, the challenge for CDFW's wildlife officers has never been greater. ✽

AFTERWORD

JUST THE FACTS: THE SCARCITY OF LAW ENFORCEMENT ON OUR NATION'S WILDLANDS

BY JAMES A. SWAN, PH.D.

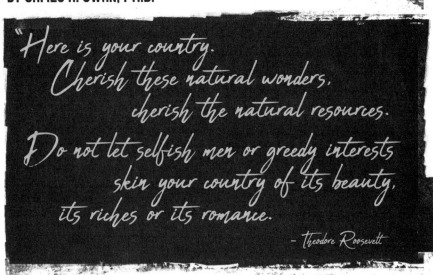

"Here is your country. Cherish these natural wonders, cherish the natural resources. Do not let selfish men or greedy interests skin your country of its beauty, its riches or its romance.

— Theodore Roosevelt

In 1960, President Dwight D. Eisenhower created the Outdoor Recreation Resources Review Commission (ORRRC) to survey current use of wildlands for recreation and make estimates for future needs. In 1962, an ORRRC report found that about 90 percent of Americans participated in at least one outdoor-recreation activity. The commission predicted that, by 2000, there would be an outdoor-recreation crisis, with many more people enjoying outdoor sports.

Today, the actual number of outdoor recreationists has increased slightly, but since 1960, the U.S. population has almost doubled. Meanwhile, the percentage of the population who enjoy some kind of outdoor recreation has plummeted to slightly below 50 percent. That's not good for the country, or its people, especially considering most people now use TVs, smartphones, personal computers, etc. at least seven hours a day. Some say we live in the "Information Age." Sociologist Barry Glassner says it's more accurate to say that we live in "A Culture of Fear," as news media have become 10 to 17 times more negative and sensational.

The use of electronic media has drawn us away from natural areas and fueled addictions to cope with anxiety. "Uppers" like methamphetamine get us high, while opioids and marijuana mellow us out. In addition, over-eating and sitting too much has resulted in an epidemic of obesity.

We need to get more people outdoors into natural areas. But as this book so vividly describes, our wildlands have become hotspots for crime.

If you haven't heard about what you've just read, blame the media. Every day, sensationalist media groups shower us with stories about crime and violence. Actually, crime has been declining nationwide over the last 25 years. However, during the same period, crime and violence have been quietly — yet significantly — increasing in state and federal forests, wildlife refuges, national monuments and parks.

Currently, there are more than 865,000 full-time and 44,000 part-time sworn federal, state and local law enforcement officers in the United States. That's almost 400 officers per 100,000 people. Urban areas have the most officers per capita. Local police departments are the largest employer of sworn officers, accounting for about 60 percent of the total.

HOW MANY OFFICERS ARE ON PATROL IN WILDLANDS?

- **GAME WARDENS** – Nationwide, there are about 6,600.
- **U.S. FISH AND WILDLIFE SERVICE** – There are about 140 uniformed wildlife inspectors at airports, seaports and borders. In addition, there are rangers for the 560 National Wildlife Refuges and 261 covert special agents.
- **NATIONAL PARK SERVICE** – Rangers, park police and special agents enforce state and federal laws in 409 sites, covering more than 84 million acres, in every U.S. state and territory. In 2005, there were 1,548 full-time National Park

Service rangers and 671 seasonal rangers. By 2014, there were only 1,322 full-time rangers and special agents, and fewer than 400 seasonal rangers.

- **NATIONAL OCEANOGRAPHIC AND ATMOSPHERIC ADMINISTRATION** – In 2012, NOAA had 114 special agents, 22 enforcement officers and 29 investigative/enforcement support positions. NOAA's jurisdiction covers more than 3 millions square miles of ocean and more than 85,000 miles of U.S. coastline, plus 13 National Marine Sanctuaries and two Marine National Monuments.
- **ARMY CORPS OF ENGINEERS** – There are 1,500 rangers manning the ACOE's 609 artificial lakes and recreation areas. Most don't carry firearms.
- **BUREAU OF LAND MANAGEMENT** – The BLM manages more than 247.3 million acres of public lands, yet only 200 rangers are available to enforce agency regulations. Another 100 special agents do long-term investigations. Since 1993, assaults on BLM lands have increased by 30 percent, vandalism has increased by 70 percent, drug manufacturing and marijuana growing have increased by 50 percent and car thefts have increased by 20 percent.
- **U.S. FOREST SERVICE** – The USFS manages 154 national forests and 20 national grasslands, encompassing 193 million acres. The USFS has about 590 uniformed law enforcement officers and 250 undercover special agents. This is down from 660 officers a few years ago.

More crime and fewer officers mean it's increasingly dangerous to be a wildlands law enforcement officer. According to the FBI, state game wardens are seven times more likely to be assaulted by a deadly weapon than any other law enforcement officer, and they suffer injuries from assaults more than twice as often as other law enforcement officers. Another study found that wardens were three times more likely to be assaulted with a weapon than other law enforcement officers. Since 1886, 284 wildlife officers from 65 agencies have been killed in the line of duty.

In Virginia, another study of game wardens' reports found that when issuing citations, conservation officers must use force eight times more frequently than other officers. In addition, 46 percent of the attacks on officers resulted in reported injuries to the officers. The study also found that wildlife officers drew firearms on suspects about four times more often than state police.

Just who are game wardens?

Game wardens, or conservation officers as they're also known, outnumber all other wildlands law enforcement officers, and they work with other federal agencies.

In California, game wardens have more responsibilities than any other state or federal law enforcement officer. In addition to wildlife laws, wardens enforce all criminal, traffic and civil laws, perform search-and-rescue operations, control nuisance animals, help wildlife biologists and do their own CSI. They're also deputy U.S. Marshals, enabling them to pursue suspects over state lines and enforce all federal laws. On call 24/7, wardens often work from a home office because they work in remote areas. They typically work alone in backcountry areas with no immediate backup. This is one reason why California game wardens carry two handguns (one visible, another concealed), a .308 rifle and a shotgun.

Game wardens also have extended powers to search autos and personal belongings, because where they work it's not always possible to get a search warrant. Plus, some wildlife laws pertain to ownership — how many shotgun shells you are carrying, how many fish or birds you may have in possession, etc. Wardens also may venture onto private lands without a search warrant, due to "exigent circumstances" because the public owns the wildlife.

In addition to the agencies already noted, the Drug Enforcement Administration (DEA) has about 4,890 special agents. The Bureau of Alcohol, Tobacco and Firearms (ATF) has about 2,400 agents. The Border Patrol, which patrols 1,900 miles of border with Mexico and more than 5,000 miles of border with Canada, has about 22,000 agents. Game wardens work with all of them.

As *Hidden War* clearly shows, game warden roles have evolved to combat illegal marijuana grows on wildlands. According to federal law, it's illegal to grow or possess cannabis unless you have special medical and legal permission. Nonetheless, 33 states currently allow the use of marijuana in some form, and 10 states and the District of Columbia allow recreational use.

California was the first state to legalize medical marijuana in 1996, and in November 2016, California voters passed Proposition 64, legalizing recreational cannabis use. For adults over 21 in California, it's now legal to use, possess and share cannabis, as well as grow a few plants at home. Recreational sales became legal in 2018. But this didn't stop the black market. Black market weed is cheaper than legal marijuana, it's not taxed and buyers can't be easily challenged for possession.

Black market marijuana is thriving in the Golden State. The Siskiyou County Sheriff has declared a "state of emergency," due to trespass marijuana gardens. In nearby Humboldt County, about 2,300 permits have been issued to grow legal pot, but authorities estimate there are more than 12,000 illegal grows in that county. And law enforcement reports that it has found records of a national network of black market pot sales.

Marijuana is grown illegally in all 50 states, but the largest illegal grows are found in California. California's illegal pot crop is conservatively estimated to be worth $14 billion a year.

Other states with significant cartel gardens on state and federal lands include Colorado, Oregon, Michigan, Wisconsin, Texas and Kentucky.

In 2016, illegal marijuana sales in the United States were estimated at $46.6 billion, with black market sales accounting for 87 percent of all sales. By comparison, in 2016, U.S. wine sales were $38 billion, corn sales were $23.3 billion and wheat sales were $7.5 billion.

The biggest illegal grows are on regional, state and federal forests, parks and wildlife refuges. Trespass grows can also be found on private lands. Eradication of these grows falls under the jurisdiction of game wardens, as well as other federal and state agencies, but state and federal agencies are shrinking. Like it or not, game wardens are caught in the middle of this war.

Three states now have tactical game warden units: Texas, Florida and California. California's MET is the first and only full-time conservation agency tactical team dedicated to stopping clandestine marijuana cultivations. This book clearly demonstrates its importance.

Hidden War gives you a good idea of what's going on, but the best way to understand what game wardens are really up against is to ride along with them. During our filming of a documentary about California's game warden shortage, and during filming for *Wild Justice* — the first game warden reality TV show, on the National Geographic channel — my son and I experienced firsthand what it's like to walk into a trespass grow. It's like being in a war zone.

When we interviewed residents of Mendocino County about trespass grows, 10 of 15 people said they'd been shot at while picking berries, riding horses, fishing, hunting or just walking in the woods. Most farmers and ranchers in that area are armed, and many wear Kevlar vests when they venture into the woods.

CDFW's MET conservatively estimates that 6,000 to 10,000 people are currently employed by cartels to run trespass grows. "At least 85 percent of the trespass growers apprehended by the MET are here illegally from south of the border," author Lt. John Nores says. CDFW's MET is an example of what may be needed nationwide to adequately fight cartel growers. Almost 4 million plants are removed from illegal grows on public lands nationwide each year, and this is estimated to be less than 20 percent of what's actually out there.

I hope this book has made you motivated, and maybe even mad. What can you do?

1. Support legislation to put more state and federal law enforcement officers into our wildlands.

2. The next time that you're outside in a natural area, keep an eye out for warning signs of a grow: a trail where there shouldn't be one, voices coming from unusual places, semi-permanent camps, lines of black plastic piping, armed individuals outside of hunting season, and fertilizers, pesticides, trash and small propane bottles scattered around. If you find something suspicious, quietly exit the area and report it immediately. Every state has a tip hotline where people can receive a reward if they report a crime and it leads to an arrest.

3. Cleaning up public lands where people have manufactured drugs, cultivated marijuana and dumped trash can run $10,000 an acre or more. Conservation groups can volunteer their time to help wardens keep the woods safe and clean. Winter is the perfect time to do this. ❀

[1] http://blog.odmp.org/2010/11/conservation-law-enforcement-more.html

[2] https://www.researchgate.net/publication/247748618_Force_Against_and_by_Game_Wardens_In_Citizen_Encounters

[3] http://www.newsweek.com/2018/01/19/mexican-drug-cartels-taking-over-california-legal-marijuana-775665.html

[4] https://www.redding.com/story/news/local/2017/10/04/siskiyou-sheriff-sessions-you-should-concerned-our-pot-state-emergency/731863001

[5] http://www.madriverunion.com/humboldt-land-of-15000-grows/

[6] https://oag.ca.gov/sites/all/files/agweb/pdfs/toc/report_2014.pdf

[7] http://beta.latimes.com/politics/la-pol-ca-marijuana-surplus-export-20171001-story.html#nt=oft12aH-1gp2

[8] https://www.inc.com/Tango-yakowicz/marijuana-sales-2016-50-billion.html

[9] http://jamesswan.com/snowgoose/wardendoc.html

[10] http://channel.nationalgeographic.com/wild-justice/

[11] http://sacramento.cbslocal.com/2013/11/05/mexican-drug-cartels-extending-violent-reach-into-calaveras-county-ranchers-property

GAME WARDEN FAQ

BY JAMES A. SWAN, PH.D.

WHAT ARE GAME WARDENS CALLED?

State game wardens are known by various names, such as conservation officers, conservation police, game wardens, wildlife enforcement agents, fish wardens, environmental police, and fish and game wardens, just to name a few. Some are also deputy federal marshals.

WHAT DO WARDENS DO?

No matter what you call them, the jobs of game wardens are basically the same: to protect public fish, wildlife and natural resources by enforcing wildlife laws, and much more. Game wardens cover the largest jurisdiction of any state or local law enforcement officer. Their varied tasks fall under criminal law, civil law, traffic law, search and rescue, environmental education, and hunter education. They are a little like modern day versions of the local sheriff in the days of the Old West.

In California, a fish and game warden must have at least two years of post-secondary education. After passing a rigorous exam, a warden will train for 16 months. Training includes wildlife law, report writing, firearms law, recognition of sporting goods gear, arrest and defense tactics, patrol techniques, search and rescue, drug and narcotics enforcement, accident investigations, arrest techniques, first aid/CPR, interview and interrogation, emergency vehicle operation, legal codes, weapons, weaponless defense, batons, fitness and much more. This is tough training. As many as half the cadets drop out before completing their training.

If they choose to stay with it, being a game warden means working from a home office, being on duty 24/7 and patrolling remote areas. This work is often alone and without backup, while using pick-ups, snowmobiles, planes, boats, ATV, underwater with SCUBA gear, horseback, bikes and foot to get around. Game wardens also perform all their own crime scene investigation. Canine companions are increasingly popular.

Almost all people contacted by wardens are armed with guns or knives, or both. Planes and trucks have been and are hit by gunfire. Wardens routinely contact and arrest armed convicted felons, with little or no back-up, in remote areas. At least 90% of public contacts on the job are nonviolent, but federal statistics show that game wardens and DEA agents have the highest risk of death on the job. Nationwide, at least 229 wildlife officers were killed or died while on duty.

All wardens are also hunter education instructors. They teach people to use firearms, which is a dramatic departure from other law enforcement officers usually discouraging firearms use. When on patrol in hunting season, everyone wardens encounter is armed. The only other time a law enforcement person meets so many armed people in the field is the military police.

It's little wonder that wardens in California are issued two .40 caliber pistols, a 12-gauge shotgun, a .308 semi-auto rifle, pepper spray, handcuffs and TASERs.

HOW MANY FEDERAL AND STATE WILDLANDS LAW ENFORCEMENT OFFICERS ARE ON PATROL?

Federal Agencies

- The U.S. Fish and Wildlife Service employs 140 uniformed wildlife inspectors at airports, sea ports and borders; roughly 500 special agents; and refuge rangers for the 560 National Wildlife Refuges.

- National Park Service rangers, park police and special agents enforce state and federal laws on 409 areas covering more than 84 million acres in every state and U.S. territories. In 2005, there were 1,548 full-time National Park Service rangers and 671 seasonal rangers. By 2014, there were 1,322 full-time rangers and special agents, and less than 400 seasonal rangers.

- In 2012, the National Oceanographic and Atmospheric Administration had 114 special agents, 22 enforcement officers and 29 investigative /enforcement support positions. Their jurisdiction covers three millions square miles of ocean and more than 85,000 miles of U.S. coastline, plus 13 National Marine Sanctuaries and two Marine National Monuments.

- At the Army Corps of Engineers, 1,500 rangers patrol 609 made-made lakes and recreation areas for the entire U.S. Most don't carry firearms.

- The Bureau of Land Management (BLM) administers more than 247.3 million acres of public lands with 200 rangers to enforce agency regulations. A hundred more special agents do long-term investigations. Since 1993, assaults on BLM lands increased by 30%, vandalism increased 70%, drug manufacturing increased by 50% and car thefts increased 20%.

- The U.S. Forest Service manages 154 national forests and 20 national grasslands that encompass 193 million acres, with about 590 uniformed law enforcement officers and 250 undercover special agents.

STATE WARDEN NUMBERS

Nationwide, there are about as many state game wardens as the New York City Police Department assigns to cover New Year's Eve celebrations: 7,000.

The following chart summarizes the numbers of game wardens in the United States and Canada. It was compiled with the assistance of the North American Wildlife Officers Association.

NUMBERS OF GAME WARDENS – IN THE FIELD FOR THE UNITED STATES		
	FEBRUARY, 2008	2017
Alabama	139	140
Alaska	96	80
Arizona	86	89
Arkansas	161	186
California	192	360
Colorado	135	224
Connecticut	57	80
Delaware	28	30
Florida	722	853
Georgia	211	200
Hawaii	120	90
Idaho	88	90
Illinois	144	120
Indiana	206	214
Iowa	83	120
Kansas	69	110
Kentucky	157	110
Louisiana	240	214
Maine	124	130
Maryland	238	254
Massachusetts	100	90
Michigan	141	200
Minnesota	154	183
Mississippi	165	198
Missouri	167	143
Montana	101	100
Nebraska	60	58
Nevada	31	40
New Hampshire	42	42
New Jersey	54	46
New Mexico	67	95

New York	264	390
North Carolina	209	350
North Dakota	35	70
Ohio	88	130
Oklahoma	118	150
Oregon	119	120
Pennsylvania	136	135
Rhode Island	35	30
South Carolina	261	261
South Dakota	61	110
Tennessee	181	235
Texas	494	470
Utah	65	70
Vermont	40	40
Virginia	150	230
Washington	138	150
West Virginia	126	126
Wisconsin	151	204
Wyoming	59	80
TOTAL WARDENS	**7,096**	**8,140**

Note: it's heartening to see the number of game wardens increasing. Perhaps the increasing number is associated with TV shows, like Wild Justice, and the half a dozen others currently airing, which introduced audiences to game wardens and the work they do.

However, there is a disheartening statistic, too. By 2024, the Bureau of Labor Statistics predicts there will only be 6,300 game wardens nationwide, despite the rising general population. Clearly, that is a matter of great concern for the conservation of wildlands and wildlife, as well as the safety of outdoor recreationists.

HISTORY OF CALIFORNIA FISH AND WILDLIFE GAME WARDENS

With 159,000 square miles of land, California is home to more than 36 million people, 1,100 miles of coastline, about 222,000 square miles of ocean waters, 30,000 miles of rivers and streams, 4,800 lakes and reservoirs, 80 major rivers, deserts, mountains and urban areas, all of which game wardens cover.

California was admitted to Union in 1850. Game wardens were the first sworn state police officers — more than 50 years before the California Highway Patrol was established. The first game wardens were deputy commissioners of the state Fish Commission in 1871. A decade later, Jack

London switched from poaching oysters to becoming a game warden, chasing down criminals in his sloop and writing a popular book about it: Tales of the Fish Patrol.

By 1901, California employed 50 game wardens. The daily creel limit of trout and the daily bag limits for ducks and doves were also 50. By 1907, the state warden force expanded to 73. In 1913, the first state fishing license issued. It cost $1.00 for residents. The same year, two wardens were killed and three others were wounded in the line of duty.

By 1949, there were 194 enforcement personnel, and in 1959, game wardens were granted full law enforcement status. They were not issued firearms and handcuffs until 1974.

The warden force reached 280 in the field in 1998. Then it shrunk to 192 in 2008. Thanks to the documentary, *Endangered Species: CA Fish and Game Wardens*, and the *Wild Justice* TV show that ran from 2010 to 2013 on the National Geographic Channel, there now are 360 — which is still the lowest per capita in the U.S.

About 10 wardens are assigned to the special operations unit, which does undercover work on felony conspiracy cases involving commercializing wildlife. They may work a case for a year or more, and are convincing actors.

Due to the shortage of game wardens in California, in addition to the marijuana groves on public wildlands, there is currently a thriving black market in fish and wildlife trafficking worth an estimated $100 million a year. This activity involves mafia, Russian mob, street gangs, drug manufacturers and users, and drug cartels.

WHAT PENALTIES RESULT FROM WILDLIFE LAW VIOLATIONS?

Many people assume the citations for wildlife law violations are slaps on the wrist. For minor infractions, the penalties are not large. However, in California, where organized crime is so significant in wildlife crime, the penalties increase as the seriousness of the crime increases. When someone commits a crime involving selling something to someone else, it becomes felony conspiracy. A suspect convicted of a felony conspiracy charge is subject to a maximum of three years in prison and a minimum $20,000 to $40,000 fine. Confiscations of cars, computers, boats, motors, firearms, gear, and the loss of hunting/fishing licenses, are always possible. And, when wardens enforce criminal laws, the penalties of those arrested and convicted are the same as if these people were arrested by other police.

SPECIAL HAZARDS FACED BY GAME WARDENS

During the two years while we produced the documentary, Endangered Species: California Fish and Game Wardens, we talked with wardens around the state about the job. I've worked with law enforcement at the local, state and federal level since the 1970s. All police work is dangerous, but the range of hazards for the Thin Green Line seemed like the largest of any group. I kept a list of some of the special hazards faced by game wardens. They include:

- Home and family are exposed, as most work from a home office
- Wardens normally work alone
- Work in uncontrolled environments
- Radio dispatch and cell-phone service dead zones are routine
- Difficulty for warden to describe their location for backup
- Traverse uneven ground by foot – mud, water, rocks, mountains, desert sands, cliffs, heavy vegetation
- Surveillances and patrol in poison oak
- Rattlesnakes, scorpions
- Heavy exposure to mosquitoes and West Nile Virus
- Firearms – wardens inspect and seize more guns than any other agency
- Discover and recover many disguised and concealed weapons
- Encounters with criminals carrying rifles and shotguns
- Bullet-resistant vests do not stop bullets from rifles
- Backup from another warden or other officer is minimal or none
- Routine work in adverse weather conditions (snow, floods, storms)
- Crossing fences on foot, mostly barbed wire
- Flying fishhooks, stray bullets and shotgun pellets
- Extended surveillances
- Surveillance in adverse topography for hours (lying in mud, hot and dry deserts, etc.)
- On the job injuries common
- Wearing cumbersome waders or other specialized protective clothing
- High exposure to sunlight (skin cancer among wardens is common)

- Hazardous material sampling for water pollution cases
- Use of specialized vehicles and boats, and associated hazards
- Work longer hours
- Boarding vessels on open ocean waters multiple times daily
- During marine patrols, backup is usually only U.S. military
- Enforce multi-crime incidents
- Difficult to be anonymous (some wardens are the only representative officer for an entire county)
- General public can knock on warden's home door or call for various reasons any hour of the day or night
- Patrol the most densely populated cities as well as the most remote areas of California
- Wardens are more likely to be assaulted during their careers that any other type of officer
- Wardens patrol behind locked gates on large land holdings where other agencies are restricted from going
- Wardens patrol county, state, federal and private lands.
- Unsafe hunting practices put wardens at risk.
- Wardens contact more persons using firearms and while under the influence of alcohol than any other law enforcement officer.
- Wardens routinely trail and subdue wounded and or diseased wild animals, including bears and mountain lions

BITES FROM DOMESTIC AND WILD ANIMALS

According to the FBI, state game wardens are seven times more likely to be assaulted by a deadly weapon than any other law enforcement officer. Park Service rangers are 12 times more likely to be assaulted than police.

HOW CAN THE PUBLIC HELP GAME WARDENS?

One way to give the wardens a hand is to report poaching and polluting. Each state and Canadian province has a 24-hour hotline for reporting poachers and polluters. If you see someone committing a wildlife crime, report them. If your tip leads to an arrest, you will get a reward. To find the hotline for your state or province, visit naweoa.org/us-ogt-tip.

TO LEARN MORE ABOUT CALIFORNIA FISH AND GAME WARDENS

- California Fish and Game Wardens Association -- cfgwa.com
- DVD -- Endangered Species: California Fish and Game Wardens, 66-minutes, narrated by Jameson Parker, 2009. http://jamesswan.com/snowgoose/wardendoc.html
- Episodes of the Wild Justice documentary series on National Geographic Channel can be found online
  - https://video.nationalgeographic.com/video/wild-justice
- North American Wildlife Enforcement Officers Association -- http://www.naweoa.org/
- North American Game Warden Museum -- http://gamewardenmuseum.org/

ECOLOGICAL IMPACTS ACROSS THE LANDSCAPE: TRESPASS MARIJUANA CULTIVATION ON WESTERN PUBLIC LANDS

BY GRETA M. WENGERT, MOURAD W. GABRIEL, J. MARK HIGLEY, AND CRAIG THOMPSON

Marijuana cultivation in California: it is a phrase that conjures up images ranging from a back-to-the-earth movement that brought people closer to the land, to pot-smoking college students, to the influx of out-of-towners to small Northern California towns looking for a piece of the vast profits being generated in the drug trade. But only recently has this phrase also come to represent an even darker side to the industry, the less well-known drawbacks to an otherwise-booming industry. This darker side is the broad assemblage of environmental impacts this industry has had and continues to have on the lands and natural resources of California and other western states. Water diversions, wildlife poisonings, and clearing of habitats are now understood to be common at cultivation sites throughout California. Going more unnoticed are the covert, less-visible ecological disturbances unique to marijuana cultivation hidden within California's vast public lands. Though many of the same clear hazards exist both in the more evident quasi-legal grows occurring on private parcels as well as in the "trespass" grows littering the public landscape, there are stark differences in the nature, detectability, and expanse of impacts between the two. When considered at the regional scale across hundreds of trespass cultivation sites on California's public and tribal lands each year, the cumulative impacts could be substantial but are, as yet, largely unexplored. Furthermore, a large portion of sites that exist on public lands are not even discovered, so the vast majority are unremediated, leaving behind a legacy of environmental damage. This chapter's aim is to describe the landscape-scale impacts and consider the cumulative influences that direct as well as indirect and more covert environmental impacts might have across the California public landscape.

IDENTIFYING THE EXTENT AND DISTRIBUTION OF TRESPASS GROW SITES ON PUBLIC LANDS

Law enforcement agencies estimate that each year between 200,000 and 500,000 illegally grown marijuana plants are detected and eradicated on California's public lands. These numbers stem from no more than several hundred law enforcement-discovered sites per year. Moreover, there are hundreds of additional marijuana grow sites spread across much of California's public and tribal lands that go undetected. Newly established sites sprout up each year, such that cumulatively, there are many thousands of active, eradicated, and abandoned grow sites in California's national forests, national and state parks, national recreation areas, and state wildlife areas at the time of this writing (Figure 2.1). Though recent media suggests that the number of grow sites on public lands has already peaked and every year since 2011 has seen the discovery of fewer and fewer public-land sites, these observations must consider the ever-decreasing support that law enforcement agencies receive to conduct surveillance to even detect these sites. Lack of support and its resulting reduction in effort for detection of sites thus falsely portrays a decreasing trend in cultivation frequency and intensity on public lands. Most daunting is the estimate that law enforcement likely detects fewer than half of the active marijuana cultivation sites each year, and of those detected, fewer than 10 percent are reclaimed or restored to their natural state. With statistics such as this, it is surprising that this issue gets so little media attention in California, much less outside of the western United States, the region within which most of California's marijuana supply flows.

The uncertainty surrounding the true number and distribution of trespass marijuana grow sites on public lands in California makes it difficult to accurately describe the extent of environmental impacts and develop solutions to reverse the problem. Some efforts to model probable areas of marijuana cultivation based on environmental and/or anthropogenic variables have shown potential in predicting likely grow site locations and distribution. A study investigating the habitat and social correlates of trespass marijuana cultivation in national parks in the southern Sierra Nevada used locations of twelve and eighty-four known cultivation sites between 2000 and 2008 in Yosemite and Sequoia-Kings Canyon National Parks, respectively, to model areas that are most likely at risk for trespass marijuana cultivation (Partelow 2008). Though the model performed well, the study fell short of indicating which variables were more or less correlated with cultivation risk in the national parks. The study, however, highlighted the major concern about risks to natural and cultural resources from this illicit activity; this was the first published documentation of concern about the environmental risks from fertilizers and pesticides used in marijuana cultivation. Despite this publication, most of California's natural-resource managers and researchers are not aware of the depth and importance of this issue. Models predicting the distribution of cultivation sites used environmental and human-related variables to identify spatial risk in Mexico (Medel and Lu 2014), although no mention is made as to any detrimental impacts to the environment from these illegal cultivation sites or what

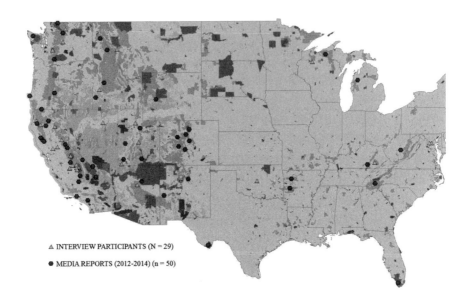

△ INTERVIEW PARTICIPANTS (N = 29)

● MEDIA REPORTS (2012-2014) (n = 50)

land ownership these sites occupied. A modeling effort specifically focused on estimating cultivation site likelihood throughout the forested regions of California and southwestern Oregon and its overlap with habitat of sensitive wildlife species is still in the accuracy assessment phase, but preliminary results suggest that there is significant overlap between high-quality habitat for the fisher (*Pekania pennanti*), a candidate for the federal Endangered Species Act, and the federally threatened northern spotted owl (*Strix occidentalis caurina*) and regions with high likelihood of trespass cultivation (Wengert et al., unpublished data). Analyses are ongoing to assess overlap with other species of conservation concern, including the Humboldt marten (*Martes caurina humboldtensis*) and cold water refugia for impacted salmonid runs. This modeling project is the first assessment of landscape-scale marijuana cultivation risk and overlap with species of conservation concern and the habitats on which they depend.

ENVIRONMENTAL IMPACTS OF TRESPASS MARIJUANA CULTIVATION ON PUBLIC LANDS

In the final chapter of John Nores' *War in the Woods*, a personal account about California's fight with trespass marijuana cultivation (which he updated in his chapter in this volume), Nores describes the environmental atrocities regularly seen at the cultivation sites that law enforcement eradicates. But he also laments the fact that so few are cleaned-up following interdiction (Nores and Swan 2010). Furthermore, the author cites water pollution, streambed alteration, littering, and poaching as significant problems needing to be addressed. Unfortunately, the presence and threat of these impacts were not generally known until recently, when independent researchers and some agency biologists began investigating anomalies in the wildlife populations they were actively monitoring (see Higley and Thompson chapters, this volume). Even then, it took several years to compile the anecdotal and evidence-based reports of wildlife mortality due to rodenticides at cultivation sites into a cumulative account of the landscape distribution of rodenticide impacts in California (Gabriel et al. 2012; Thompson et al. 2013; Gabriel et al. 2015). Since then, our understanding of the environmental impacts associated with this illicit activity has grown significantly due to focused investigations at cultivation sites and the areas surrounding them. The information that is available, however, consists of preliminary findings and anecdotal reports from which cumulative impacts can only be approximated.

A program collecting detailed information from trespass cultivation sites on public and tribal lands is in its infancy; it currently consists mainly of data from approximately fifty sites throughout California and southern Oregon, but all of these are primarily located in Northern California (Humboldt, Trinity, and Plumas Counties). In addition, researchers have collected a limited amount of information from sites within the southern Sierra Nevada, but these consist mainly of casual observations of the chemicals and fertilizers found during the reclamation process (Gabriel et al. 2013). For example, in the remediation of hundreds of cultivation sites throughout the foothills and mid-elevation slopes of the southern Sierra Nevada, lead reclamation specialist Shane Krogen suggested there was seldom a site he encountered that did not have anticoagulant rodenticides (AR) present. These hundreds of sites occurred in only two of California's national forests and excluded those occurring within the two adjacent national parks (the National Park Service generally conducts its own eradication and reclamation efforts). It is generally accepted, and law enforcement data supports, that all national forests in California whose climates and vegetation characteristics make the cultivation of marijuana feasible, experience comparable frequencies and densities of trespass cultivation sites.

Investigations and mapping of several cultivation sites from 2013 and 2015 have preliminary estimates of actual plant patch footprints at an average of over one acre. Based on anecdotal observations over the past several years, however, the spatial orientation and distribution of plant patches within the cultivation complexes appear to be shifting from a small number of large, expansive patches to networks of many small, disjunct patches scattered across a much larger overall footprint on the landscape. How this change will manifest in terms of impacts to wildlife, water, and other resources is unclear, but the notably larger footprint of rodenticide, pesticide, fertilizer, and water use likely equates to a greater cumulative, landscape-level impact, and certainly spreads its impacts to an area significantly greater than the acre of grow patch typically observed. Undoubtedly, plant patches scattered throughout a watershed have the ability to dewater multiple streams or springs, and the run-off from these more dispersed patches has greater potential and capacity to contaminate more of the watershed than a solitary larger patch on a single hillside.

Rodenticides (including ARs, neurotoxic rodenticides, and cholecalciferol compounds, which calcify the internal organs) are the cause of environmental impacts and likely have received the most scientific focus and media attention due to their causing mortality in a high-profile species being considered for listing under the federal Endangered Species Act (Gabriel et al. 2012; Gabriel et al. 2015; Thompson et al. 2013; see also Chapters 3 and 4 in this volume). These compounds are found at a majority of trespass marijuana cultivation sites investigated in California (Gabriel et al., unpublished data). With an average mass of 10 pounds per site, these toxicants are spread across all the plant patches and water cisterns associated with a trespass grow, along the irrigation lines feeding the site, and around the camps at which the growers live throughout the growing season (typically from April through September). Finally, many of these toxicants are housed in water-resistant containers, thus allowing long periods of time or the disturbance by an animal to compromise containers.

The cumulative effects of such unregulated and widespread use can be substantial. Animals either die directly from ingestion of the poisoned bait or die through secondary poisoning by consuming other animals that have ingested the baits. Rodents survive up to several days with the poisons in their systems, leave the cultivation areas, and therefore pose risks to carnivores and raptors well outside the footprints of the grow patches where the rodenticides are distributed. For instance, in our prey abundance sampling at grow and control sites in 2015, we inadvertently captured a mountain quail (*Oreortyx pictus*) in our control site (almost 2 km from the nearest known grow site) that tested positive for AR exposure. In addition, we know the residual impacts of AR at grow sites can last many months after eradication because the majority of rodents captured at grow sites that were tested were positive for AR exposure 6–12 months after the site was eradicated and several months after the sites were remediated (Wengert et al., unpublished data). Furthermore, in a study of the fisher, a forest-obligate species, researchers found that 85 percent of all tested fishers were exposed to AR in a northwestern California population and in two populations in the southern Sierra Nevada (Gabriel et al. 2015). Unfortunately, this percentage rose higher from an earlier study in which the researchers found no spatial pattern to the exposures, meaning AR exposure was ubiquitous throughout the fisher's range within the study areas (Gabriel et al. 2012).

Research investigating how these rodenticides impact the prey communities on which so many sensitive forest carnivore and raptors depend already suggests that prey diversity and populations are depressed at many of the sites (Wengert et al., unpublished data). Furthermore, there is evidence that ARs can bioaccumulate in invertebrates because they lack the clotting mechanisms upon which ARs act, making ARs nonlethal. It is unknown how quickly invertebrates metabolize these compounds, but they likely pose risks to countless other species that prey on ground-dwelling invertebrates for extended periods of time.

The pesticides placed throughout the plant patches and along irrigation lines also leach into the soil. Several types of AR and carbofuran (a particularly hazardous pesticide notoriously used to kill lions in Africa as well as numerous other species worldwide (Richards 2011)) have been detected in soil within plant patches in several sites in Northern California (Gabriel and Wengert, unpublished data). Residual chemicals such as these remaining in the soil when the wet season arrives will get mobilized and washed into the watersheds. Consequently, pesticides used at grow sites have been detected by water sampling equipment placed in headwater streams just below grow sites (Gabriel and Wengert, unpublished data). One pesticide in particular, Diazinon, was found in stream water sampled just below three different grow sites in northwestern California (Gabriel and Wengert, unpublished data). This pesticide is acutely toxic to most insects so theoretically is impacting aquatic macroinvertebrate communities on which so many other aquatic species depend, but these potential impacts are just now starting to be investigated.

Aside from the vast direct and indirect effects of the illegal overuse of toxicants at nearly all trespass grow sites in California, growers also use all kinds of high-nutrient fertilizers in copious volumes, far exceeding the needs of the plants and soil area. The amounts of fertilizer we discovered at each trespass grow site during our investigations between 2012 and 2015 in Northern California and in the northern Sierra Nevada ranged from about 300 pounds to over 4,300 pounds of dry, soluble fertilizer distributed across single small patches or several large patches spanning hundreds of meters of creek drainage. In 2010, the US Forest Service conducted a massive eradication and cleanup effort on the Sequoia and Sierra National Forests, removing 5.4 tons of unused fertilizer from sixty-five trespass grow sites. This effort was conducted in August and September, after the growing season, meaning these 5.4 tons represented the *leftover* fertilizer (Thompson, unpublished data). Given that every site we've visited since 2012 has had vast amounts of fertilizer suggests that each of the thousands of sites strewn across California's public lands over the past decade have contributed to excessive nutrient loading to the ecosystem. One possible result of this nutrient excess is a multitude of fundamental changes to soil fertility across large swaths of the landscape. Preliminary results of nitrogen-fixing microbial diversity indicate significant differences between grow patches and nearby control patches (Siering

Distribution of illegal trespass marijuana cultivation sites on public, tribal and private/industrial lands in California between 2004 and 2014.

and Wengert, unpublished data). Consider a short 25 km stretch of the South Fork of the Trinity River having at least twenty-six trespass grow sites within its tributaries (likely many more than that), with hundreds if not thousands of pounds of fertilizer at each. Much of this likely gets mobilized with early fall rains and ends up within the river. Concerns are that this immense influx of nutrients into the system might enhance growth of cyanobacteria, contributing to dangerous blue-green algae blooms that in turn can release microcystins posing risks to a wide array of taxa, yet another plausible threat to wildlife.

These direct threats to the forest and associated aquatic ecosystems are being investigated, and preliminary evidence is being generated to support their existence. However, there are a host of other ideas about how the activities at trespass marijuana cultivation sites might impact the forest communities in less direct ways. We have begun investigating how forest animals use the extensive network of trails that growers build within and between grow sites, in addition to the activity patterns of those animals frequenting the camps and dumps attracted by food and other olfactory attractants. Initial findings show frequent use of camps and dumps by many forest species, including black bears (*Ursus americanus*), bobcats (*Lynx rufus*), gray fox (*Urocyon cinereoargenteus*), coyotes (*Canis latrans*), ringtail (*Bassariscus astutus*), many species of rodents and hares, game species including black-tailed deer (*Odocoileus hemionus*), mountain quail and band-tailed pigeon (*Patagioenas fasciata*), and certain high-profile species such as mountain lions (*Puma concolor*) and the fisher. Furthermore, the trails growers construct are commonly traveled by mountain lions, bobcats, coyotes, black-tailed deer, and the occasional fisher. Though seemingly benign, this encouraged use of trails by different species could lead to increased chances of interaction. If interactions are more frequent between fishers and their main predators (mountain lions and bobcats), we suspect predation rates on fishers will increase, and this is important because predation is the primary source of mortality for fishers throughout California (Wengert et al. 2014).

The depression of rodent and other small prey populations brought about by extensive use of rodenticides in and surrounding grow sites likely affects the survival and fitness of the carnivore species that depend on that prey. When prey resources decline precipitously, carnivore populations typically show a behavioral or numeric response, or both, by increased home range size, lower survival, and lower reproductive success (Pereira et al. 2006; Schmidt 2008; Ferreras et al. 2011). We know that the diversity of prey and relative abundance of larger-bodied prey appear to be decreased at many grow sites (Wengert et al., unpublished data), so if this trend is common across all California trespass grow sites, carnivore populations are likely suffering the same effects. In conjunction with the intensified risks of direct poisoning at these sites, species of conservation concern such as the fisher, northern spotted owl, northern goshawk (*Accipiter gentilis*), and Humboldt marten would face cumulative perils from the many factors described above, ultimately risking population-level declines. Indeed, the United States Fish and Wildlife Service (USFWS) has proposed the fisher for listing as threatened under the federal Endangered Species Act, with rodenticides from trespass marijuana cultivation listed as one of the two main causative threats to be considered in the decision to list (USFWS 2014).

LEGACY EFFECTS, UNCERTAINTIES, AND THE REALITIES OF THE ENVIRONMENTAL DAMAGE

That said, it should be clear that the diversity, spatial extent, and cumulative effects of marijuana cultivation on public lands have the potential to be monumental and formidable. The estimate that California's national forests have seen several hundred newly established cultivation sites each year at least for the past decade is disconcerting, but the fact that a generous estimate of roughly 10 percent of sites are remediated each year underscores the reality that to this day, there are probably thousands of sites with all their associated poisons, infrastructure, and garbage still in place. Consequently, the legacy effects of these sites grow cumulatively over time, as well as across the landscape. Every year, the number of contaminated, compromised patches of forest only grows larger and the cumulative impacts just expand. The hazards of these sites dissipate slowly at best, especially due to many poisons remaining unopened in their original packaging for wildlife to tear into them.

Given the uncertainties surrounding the real number of sites on California's national forests, the changes in the characteristics of sites over time (for example, in all the sites we visited in 2015, a vast majority had carbofuran present, whereas until that year, only a handful of sites did), and the complex ways in which the environmental effects cumulatively mount up, it is difficult to quantify the enormity of this issue. Though we know each cultivation site across the forests has its own array of poisons and overuse of fertilizers, how much is actually making it into the watershed? We know that carnivores are being poisoned directly and through consumption of poisoned prey, but are the fish, amphibians, and benthic invertebrates suffering the same impacts downstream of these sites? There is evidence that prey populations are depressed at and immediately surrounding grow sites, but do they recover quickly if the sites are remediated? We suspect the answers to these questions will become evident over time as the public becomes more aware, as more investigators begin addressing these issues, and as partnerships between researchers and law enforcement continue to grow. New sites continue to stack up each year, creating a backlog of legacy impacts that will be difficult to reconcile with even the greatest public awareness and joint remediation efforts.

All that we know and do not know regarding the cumulative landscape impacts of this illicit activity on our public lands and the daunting quantity and distribution of cultivation sites can be overwhelming. Despite this reality, agencies, tribes, nongovernmental organizations (NGOs), and individual citizens are approaching this problem head-on, tackling site clean-ups wherever they can and with the little funding available. In fall of 2014, in an immense six-day effort by NGOs, California state and federal agency scientists and law enforcement officers, citizens and local tribal members, and National Guard soldiers, the chemicals, infrastructure, and garbage from ten separate sites on Six Rivers and Shasta-Trinity National Forests were removed; the total haul-out amounted to five tons of cultivation infrastructure and garbage, including several hundred pounds of fertilizer and pesticides. In another effort in 2015 with the same collaboration of participants, five sites on tribal land and ten sites on Northern California's national forest were reclaimed. But clean-ups are not limited to northern California. In 2014 a joint effort between the US Forest Service, California Department of Fish and Wildlife, and nonprofit partners remediated thirteen trespass grow sites on the Sierra and Sequoia National Forests, removing 3.5 tons of garbage, 15 miles of irrigation tubing, and over thirty containers of pesticides and rodenticides. In addition to these comprehensive, focused efforts, the multi-agency law enforcement teams tasked with locating, surveilling, and eradicating trespass cultivation sites often haul a few net loads of trash and pesticides out of many of the sites they raid, even though they are under no mandate and have no funding to do so. Though this problem may cause many a feeling of helplessness, small steps to initiate the recovery of our public lands by these partnerships are a start and can inspire the public to be more involved and aware. Likewise, more complete investigation and documentation of the scope of this problem can encourage policy makers to draft support for continued monitoring, remediation efforts, and enforcement to prevent this clandestine activity from taking root in the first place. While the forests wait for a more permanent solution to safeguard them from this ruthless invasion, these new partnerships will continue chipping away at this enduring insult to California's vast and exquisite public lands.

Editor's Note: Excerpt from Where There's Smoke (2018), edited by Char Miller, and reprinted with permission from University of Kansas Press, kansaspress.ku.edu.

WORKS CITED

Ferreras, P., A. Travaini, S. C. Zapata, and M. Delibes. 2011. "Short-Term Responses of Mammalian Carnivores to a Sudden Collapse of Rabbits in Mediterranean Spain." *Basic and Applied Ecology* 12: 116–124.

Gabriel, M. W., G. M. Wengert, J. M. Higley, S. Krogen, W. Sargent, and D. L. Clifford. 2013. "Silent Forests? Rodenticides on Illegal Marijuana Crops Harm Wildlife." *Wildlife Professional* 7: 46–50.

Gabriel, M. W., G. M. Wengert, L. W. Woods, N. Stephenson, J. M. Higley, C. Thompson, S. M. Matthews, R. A. Sweitzer, K. Purcell, R. H. Barrett, S. M. Keller, P. Gaffney, M. Jones, R. Poppenga, J. E. Foley, R. N. Brown, D. Clifford, and B. N. Sacks. 2015. "Patterns of Natural and Human-caused Mortality Factors of a Rare Forest Carnivore, the Fisher (*Pekania pennanti*) in California." PLOS ONE 10, 11: e0140640. doi:10.1371/journal.pone.0140640.

Gabriel, M. W., L. W. Woods, R. Poppenga, R. A. Sweitzer, C. Thompson, S. M. Matthews, J. Mark Higley, S. M. Keller, K. Purcell, R. H. Barrett, G. M. Wengert, B. N. Sacks, and D. L. Clifford. 2012. "Anticoagulant Rodenticides on our Public and Community Lands: Spatial Distribution of Exposure and Poisoning of a Rare Forest Carnivore." *PLOS ONE* 7, 7:e40163.

Medel, M., and Y. Lu. 2015. "Illegal Drug Cultivation in Mexico: An Examination of the Environmental and Human Factors." *Cartography and Geographic Information Science* 42, 2: 190–204. doi: 10.1080/15230406.2014.985716.

Nores, J., Jr., and J. A. Swan. 2010. *War in the Woods: Combating the Marijuana Cartels on America's Public Lands.* Guilford, CT: Globe Pequot.

Partelow, C. D. 2008. "Using GIS to Depict Resource Risk from Probable Cannabis Cultivation Sites." MA thesis, San Jose State University.

Pereira, J. A., N. G. Fracassi, M. M. Uhart. 2006. "Numerical and Spatial Responses of Geoffroy's Cat (*Oncifelis geoffroyi*) to Prey Decline in Argentina." *Journal of Mammalogy* 87: 1132–1139.

Richards, N., ed. 2011. *Carbofuran and Wildlife Poisoning: Global Perspectives and Forensic Approaches.* Hoboken, NJ: Wiley.

Schmidt, K. 2008. "Behavioural and Spatial Adaptation of the Eurasian Lynx to a Decline in Prey Availability." *Acta Theriologica* 53: 1–16.

Thompson, C. M., R. A. Sweitzer, M. W. Gabriel, K. Purcell, R. H. Barrett, and R. Poppenga. 2013. "Impacts of Rodenticide and Insecticide Toxicants from Marijuana Cultivation Sites on Fisher Survival Rates in the Sierra National Forest, California." *Conservation Letters* 7. DOI: 10.1111/conl.12038.

Wengert, G. M., M. W. Gabriel, S. M. Matthews, J. M. Higley, R. A. Sweitzer, C. Thompson, K. Purcell, R. H. Barrett, and L. W. Woods. 2014. "Using DNA to Describe and Quantify Interspecific Killing of Fishers in California." *Journal of Wildlife Management* 78: 603–611.

USFWS. 2014. Draft Species Report, Fisher (*Pekania pennanti*), West Coast Population. Washington, DC: United States Fish and Wildlife Service.

ACTIVE INGREDIENT	CATEGORY	CLASS	BRAND NAMES [FOUND AT SITES]	BIOACCUMULATION POTENTIAL[A]	MAMMAL TOXICITY[B]	BIRD TOXICITY[C]	FISH TOXICITY[D]
Acephate	Insecticide	Organophosphate	Orthonex	Low	Moderate	Moderate	Low
Aldicarb	Insecticide	Carbamate	Temik	Low	High	High	Moderate
Bifenthrin	Insecticide	Pyrethroid	Ortho Bug-B-Gone, Ortho-Klor	High	High	Moderate	High
Brodifacoum	Rodenticide	Anticoagulant	D-Con	High	High	High	High
Bromethalin	Rodenticide	Unclassified	Real Kill Rat and Mouse Killer	High	High	High	High
Carbaryl	Insecticide	Carbamate	Sevin	Low	Moderate	Moderate	Moderate
Carbofuran	Insecticide	Carbamate	Furadan	Low	High	High	Moderate
Chlorpyrifos	Insecticide	Organophosphate	Ortho Dursban	High	High	High	High
Cyfluthrin	Insecticide	Pyrethroid	Bayer Advanced Garden Insect Killer	Moderate	High	Moderate	High
Diazinon	Insecticide	Organophosphate	Ortho Diazinon	Moderate	Moderate	High	High
Diphacinone	Rodenticide	Anticoagulant	JT Eaton Gopher Poison, Tomcat Bait Chunx, Wilco Ground Squirrel Bait	High	High	Low	Moderate
d-trans Allethrin	Insecticide	Pyrethroid	Real-Kill Ant Killer	High	Moderate	Low	Moderate
Fenbutatin-oxide	Insecticide	Organotin	Orthonex	Moderate	Low	Moderate	High

ACTIVE INGREDIENT	CATEGORY	CLASS	BRAND NAMES (FOUND AT SITES)	BIOACCUMULATION POTENTIAL[a]	MAMMAL TOXICITY[b]	BIRD TOXICITY[c]	FISH TOXICITY[d]
Gamma-Cyhalothrin	Insecticide	Pyrethroid	Specracide Triazicide	High	High	Low	High
Hydramethylnon	Insecticide	trifluoromethyl aminohydrazone	Grants Ant Bait	Low	Moderate	Moderate	Moderate
Malathion	Insecticide	Organophosphate	Ortho Malathion	Low	Moderate	Moderate	High
Permethrin	Insecticide	Pyrethroid	Orthomax Garden and Landscape Insect Killer, KGRO Ready to Use Multi-Purpose Insect Killer Granules, Ortho Ant-B-Gone	Moderate	Moderate	Low	High
Phenothrin	Insecticide	Pyrethroid	Ortho Flying Insect Killer	Moderate	Low	Low	High
Pyrethrum	Insecticide	Pyrethroid	Ortho Ant-B-Gone	Low	Moderate	Low	High
Tetramethrin	Insecticide	Pyrethroid	Ortho Flying Insect Killer	Low	Low	Low	High
Tralomethrin	Insecticide	Pyrethroid	Real-Kill Ant Killer	High	High	Low	High
Triforine	Fungicide	piperazine derivative	Orthonex	Low	Low	Low	High
Zinc Phosphide	Rodenticide	Unclassified	Sure Stop Gopher Killer, Sweeney's Poison Peanuts, Grant's Gopher Killer	Low	High	High	Moderate

Source: Jeffcoach 2012.

Note: All thresholds are derived from EPA regulatory guidelines.

[a] Octanol-water partition coefficient (Log P) where < 2.7 = low bioaccumulation, 2.7–3.0 = moderate, and > 3.0 = high.

[b] Acute oral LD50 (mg kg-1) where > 2,000 = low, 100–2,000 = moderate, and < 100 = high.

[c] Acute LD50 (mg kg-1) where > 2,000 = low, 100–2,000 = moderate, and < 100 = high.

[d] Acute 96-hour LC50 (mg 1-1) where > 100 = low, 0.1–100 = moderate, and < 0.1 high.

Contact: Yating Campbell
916.445.4081

NEWS RELEASE

FOR IMMEDIATE RELEASE
JANUARY 26, 2017

K9 PHEBE CRACKS DOWN ON CARTEL CANNABIS GROWS

SACRAMENTO – California State Board of Equalization Chairwoman Fiona Ma, CPA, along with Assemblymember Jim Wood and Senator Mike McGuire presented legislative resolutions to Phebe, the amazing four-legged member and secret weapon of the California Department of Fish and Wildlife K9 unit and the Marijuana Enforcement Team, who puts her life on the line for Californians every time she catches a criminal while on duty.

With approximately 400 wildlife officers in the state patrolling 159,000 square miles of natural habitat, officers have a variety of responsibilities including catching poachers, responding to oil spills, providing public safety, educating the public, and eradicating illegal marijuana grows. Illegal marijuana cultivation sites destroy land, habitat, wildlife, and threaten the lives and safety of Californians.

With the passage of Proposition 64, demand for cannabis likely will grow and underground economic activity may grow with it. Every acre used by these illegal grows damages land and wildlife and undercuts legally licensed growers that pay taxes and follow the rules.

"Phebe plays an integral role on the Marijuana Enforcement Team, having participated in more than 580 arrest missions where more than 18 tons of processed marijuana were seized and destroyed. Last year alone, she was almost stabbed at least four times. The dangerous work she performs keeps Californians, the wildlife, and the environment safe while saving the lives of her teammates. Phebe is one of my favorite state workers, and her pension of dog bones is well deserved!" said Ma.

"All of law enforcement work incredibly hard to protect public safety, but K9 Phebe, the highly-trained secret weapon of the Department of Fish and Wildlife's Marijuana Enforcement Team, deserves our deepest gratitude for her public service," said Assemblymember Jim Wood (D-Healdsburg). "With 100 poaching cases, 100 weapon finds, tracking 175 suspects, aiding in 900 arrests and her — ouch — 112 bite apprehensions, she has had a stellar career. Thank you Phebe, may you find your retirement peaceful and full of treats."

In honor of Phebe, Front Street Animal Shelter offered free adoptions on site. Also present to help educate the public about the importance of service animals were Canine Companions for Independence and Capital City K9. ✤

Game wardens with the California Department of Fish and Game, along with the K9 Unit and K9 Phebe were honored in the California legislature for their work on the Marijuana Enforcement Team (MET).

CALIFORNIA LEGISLATURE SENATE RESOLUTION

BY THE HONORABLE MIKE MCGUIRE

2ND SENATORIAL DISTRICT; RELATIVE TO COMMENDING THE MARIJUANA ENFORCEMENT TEAM AND K9 UNIT OF THE CALIFORNIA DEPARTMENT OF FISH AND WILDLIFE

WHEREAS, The people of California have a special respect for and are daily indebted to the men and women who serve in law enforcement to protect public safety, including employees of the California Department of Fish and Wildlife (CDFW) and the members of the Department's Marijuana Enforcement Team (MET) together with its K9 Unit, whose notable heroine is K9 Phebe, a renowned dog that also has served in other notable law enforcement capacities over the course of her stellar career; and

WHEREAS, Representing the first dedicated full-time special operations conservation agency in the CDFW's distinguished 146-year history that is tasked with stopping clandestine outdoor and indoor marijuana cultivation operations throughout California, the MET began in 2013 as a pilot program and became operational on a full-time, dedicated basis in January 2014 with a team staffed by 11 officers, who include a professional canine handler, Brian Boyd, as well as the team's indispensable dog, Phebe, officially known as K9 Phebe; and

WHEREAS, By current estimates, up to 60 percent of the marijuana consumed in the United States is grown in California, and the deleterious environmental impacts of prohibited kinds of large-scale marijuana cultivation include; among other devastating consequences, the erosion of fragile soils; overloading waters, especially rivers and streams, with nutrients; the poisoning of fish and wildlife as a result of the use of rodenticides, fertilizers, and prohibited, highly toxic pesticides; and the siphoning off even scarcer water resources, as exemplified by the estimated 1.3 billion gallons of water stolen throughout the State in the 2014 and 2015 drought years for Trespass/Drug Trafficking Organization (DTO) outdoor marijuana cultivation; and

WHEREAS, Working together, the MET and K9 Unit support the Department's efforts to stop the public safety threat from DTO cultivation operations, which often involve the use of firearms to protect illegal grow sites and their illicit crops, and during the course of these often perilous missions, K9 Phebe has repeatedly played a vital role and saved the lives of MET members through her effective K9 apprehension tactics deployed in the pursuit of armed suspects, fugitive tracking and recovering operations, and evidence detection and search missions, and

Whereas, Borne out by eye-popping statistics, the remarkable success of the MET since its July 2013 inception is reflected in the 2.1 million poisoned marijuana plants and the 18 tons of processed marijuana seized and destroyed by the MET; the 745 felony arrests made and 433 firearms seized during MET missions; and the MET's removal of 335 tons of grow site waste, trash, and pollutants; 1.65 million feet-311 miles-of black poly pipe, 41 tons of fertilizers; and 368 gallons of legal and illegal toxic chemicals; and

WHEREAS, In addition, during a record-setting period of drought, the MET removed 614 water diversions/dams that had directed 748 million gallons of precious water to illegal grow sites, and through these removal operations, the MET prevented another 748 million gallons of water from being stolen for illicit cultivation; and

WHEREAS, Now in their fourth year of operation, the extremely committed members of the MET, and K9 Phebe and her handler, Brian Boyd, have made exceptional progress in the Department's steadfast efforts to protect public safety, rectify extensive environmental destruction to California's wildlife resources, and, as the State experiences an ongoing, agriculturally disastrous drought, to protect and preserve vital water assets, for all of which achievements, the MET and the K9 Unit are eminently deserving of the admiration and praise of the people of California; now, therefore, be it

RESOLVED BY SENATOR MIKE MCGUIRE, That he takes great pleasure in commending and thanking the Marijuana Enforcement Team and the K9 Unit of the California Department of Fish and Wildlife for their laudable and consequential efforts to protect the health, well-being, and safety of the State's citizenry while also protecting the State's wildlife and waterways and helping to rectify environmental damage resulting from marijuana cultivation.

Members Resolution No. 49
Dated this 26th day of January 2017
Honorable Mike McGuire
2nd Assembly District

CALIFORNIA LEGISLATURE ASSEMBLY RESOLUTION

BY THE HONORABLE JIM WOOD

2ND ASSEMBLY DISTRICT; RELATIVE TO LAUDING THE ACCOMPLISHMENTS OF K9 PHEBE

WHEREAS, The people of California have a special respect for and are daily indebted to the men and women who serve in law enforcement to protect public safety, including employees of the California Department of Fish and Wildlife (CDFW) and the members of the Department's Marijuana Enforcement Team (MET) together with its K9 Unit, whose notable heroine is K9 Phebe, a renowned dog that also has served in other notable law enforcement capacities over the course of her stellar career; and

WHEREAS, Representing the first dedicated full-time special operations conservation agency in the CDFW's distinguished 146-year history that is tasked with stopping clandestine outdoor and indoor marijuana cultivation operations throughout California, the MET became operational on a full-time, dedicated basis in January 2014 with a team staffed by 11 officers, who include a professional canine handler, Brian Boyd, as well as the team's indispensable dog, Phebe, officially known as K9 Phebe; and

WHEREAS, By current estimates, up to 70 percent of the marijuana consumed in the United States is grown in California, and the deleterious environmental impacts of prohibited kinds of large-scale marijuana cultivation include; among other devastating consequences, the erosion of fragile soils; overloading waters, especially rivers and streams, with nutrients; the poisoning of fish and wildlife as a result of the use of rodenticides, fertilizers, and prohibited, highly toxic pesticides; and the siphoning off of hundreds of millions of gallons of precious water resources; and

WHEREAS, Working together, K9 Phebe and the MET support the Department's efforts to stop the public safety threat from Drug Trafficking Organization marijuana cultivation operations, whose perpetrators frequently use firearms, including various automatic weapons and other rifles and handguns, to protect illegal grow sites and their illicit crops, and during the course of MET's often perilous missions, K9 Phebe has repeatedly played a vital role and saved the lives of various CDFW and MET staff through her effective K9 apprehension tactics deployed in the pursuit of armed suspects, fugitive tracking and recovering operations, and evidence detection and search missions, in addition to which, she has assisted during approximately 300 allied agency marijuana enforcement related operations statewide; and

WHEREAS, K9 Phebe's remarkably effective role in aiding law enforcement is further borne out by her career statistics, which include, among others, at least 100 wildlife evidence finds in the course of fish and wildlife poaching cases; approximately 100 weapons-related finds, 20 of which involved high profile murder cases; tracking about 175 felony suspects throughout the State, inclusive of 112 bite apprehensions, as well as aiding in approximately 900 additional arrests; and successfully tackling at least 25 armed suspects, and thereby protecting officers who might otherwise have been seriously injured or killed; and

WHEREAS, An exceptionally well-trained and versatile canine, K9 Phebe also has shown herself to be highly effective in helping to find lost children and adults during search and rescue operations and has contributed to vital public outreach efforts during approximately 200 school and public demonstrations held throughout the State; and

WHEREAS, Having proven herself to be an exceptional and not infrequently life-saving asset to law enforcement, K9 Phebe also has made invaluable contributions to far-reaching and consequential efforts of the CDFW and the MET to prevent further environmental destruction resulting from illicit marijuana cultivation and to protect public safety and the safety of those who work to ensure it; now, therefore, be it

RESOLVED BY ASSEMBLYMEMBER JIM WOOD, That he commends and thanks K9 Phebe and her handler Brian Boyd, the staff of the California Department of Fish and Wildlife and its Marijuana Enforcement Team, and other law enforcement officers across California with whom Phebe has worked to protect the well-being and safety of the State's citizenry.

Members Resolution No. 189
Dated this 26th day of January 2017
Honorable Jim Wood
2nd Assembly District